Istanbul - 1434 / 2013

A translation of "Asr-ı Saadet Toplumu"

Published by:

Erkam Publications

Ikitelli Organize Sanayi Bölgesi Mahallesi
Atatürk Bulvarı Haseyad 1. Kısım No: 60/3-C
Başakşehir, Istanbul, Turkey
Tel: (+90 212) 671 07 00 pbx
Fax: (+90 212) 671 07 48
E-mail: info@islamicpublishing.net
Web site: www.islamicpublishing.net

ISBN : 978-9944-83-354-7

The author : Osman Nuri Topbaş
Translator : Erdinç Atasever
Copy Editor : Suleyman Derin
Graphics : Zakir Shadmanov (Worldgraphics)
Printed by : Erkam Printhouse

The Society of the Age of Bliss

Osman Nuri Topbaş

ERKAM PUBLICATIONS

Foreword

Eternal praises and thanks to our Benevolent Lord for having made us an *ummah* of the Beloved Messenger of Allah -upon him blessings and peace- and for having presented him to humankind as the pinnacle of moral excellence!...

Eternal greetings to the Beloved Messenger of Allah -upon him blessings and peace-, as well as his family and companions, for having raised the Companions and elevated them like the stars in the skies; and also for having given humankind an unparalleled gift that is the *Asr-u Saadah*, the Age of Bliss!...

The Age of Bliss refers to an age of peace and happiness, in which human beings enjoyed the greatest joy thinkable.

The Age of Bliss were times honored by the presence of the Blessed Prophet -upon him blessings and peace- that stood witness to the revelation of the Holy Quran, the font of guidance for entire humankind. It were again those exceptional times that saw the emergence of the peerless generation of Companions, who carried the Light of Prophethood to lands and ages remote; who built a civilization of virtue, unrivaled in world history, by reaching the furthermost heights of compassion and maturity.

The term *Asr-u Saadah* has also been used, from time to time, to refer to period of the Righteous Caliphs, to the succeeding *Tabiun* generation, even to the *Tabau Tabiin* generation subsequent to it.

The Beloved Prophet -upon him blessings and peace- says:

"The best of my *ummah* are those who live in my times, then those who follow them and then those follow them…" (Bukhari, Ashabu'n-Nabi, 1)

The *Asr-u Saadah* therefore *is* the Age of Bliss, the most ideal of times. It is second to none in being the most fondly and longingly remembered period in the history of Islam.

Some exegetes comment that the vow taken on *asr*, or 'time', in *surah* al-Asr, is also in reference to the *Asr-u Saadah*; for it was during those times that the true was definitively separated from false.

From a worldly and egoistic perspective, the Age of Bliss was in no way a period of material happiness and comfort. On the contrary, it marked times of harsh living, a period filled with demanding struggles. But then again, they were also the times that stood witness to the invaluable blessings that were the life of the Noble Messenger -upon him blessings and peace- and the emergence of Islam. It was an era also in which the principles that ensured the happiness of humankind both in this world and in the Hereafter were founded. It was an age that watched on as a previously cruel, oppressive and tyrant mob of human were elevated through the truth, justice and good morals. It was an age that saw the greatest ever revolution in the history of mankind, where the dark desires of the ego were replaced by the glorious light of spirituality and in which spirits were set free from the captivity of the flesh. In short, it was an age when people began to take flight from evil towards eternal happiness.

To gain a closer acquaintance with the unique beauties of Islam which guide one from darkness into light, it is hence necessary to enter the spiritual climate of the Age of Bliss.

Dear Readers!

Our aim throughout this book, which is a compilation of various articles supplemented by some further examples, has been to ensure a better understanding of the nature of that celebrated, sacred age. To further serve this purpose and to provide a better idea of the breathtaking improvement human character has undergone since, we have tried to render our subject matter more tangible by including some examples of the innumerable scenes of virtue belonging to that age.

In this regard, I would like to extend a sincere thanks to Dr. Murat Kaya and pray to Allah, glory unto Him, to render his efforts a never-ending source of rewards.

Osman Nûri Topbaş
December 2009

بسم الله الرحمن الرحيم

وَالسَّابِقُونَ الْأَوَّلُونَ مِنَ الْمُهَاجِرِينَ وَالْأَنْصَارِ وَالَّذِينَ
اتَّبَعُوهُمْ بِإِحْسَانٍ رَضِيَ اللَّهُ عَنْهُمْ وَرَضُوا عَنْهُ

And the first to lead the way, of the Muhajirin and the Ansar, and those who followed them in goodness - Allah is well pleased with them and they are well pleased with Him, and He hath made ready for them Gardens underneath which rivers flow, wherein they will abide for ever. That is the supreme triumph.

The Society of the Age of Bliss

The Society of the Age of Bliss

During the Age of Ignorance, humankind was grounded in bleak darkness. Ignorance was deep-seated; deviancy and transgression were running rife. Chaos was relentlessly showing its ugly face. The Arabian deserts had turned into seas of blood, flowing from the wounds of never-ending blood feuds.

Justice and right always belonged to the powerful. Those who acquired power would suddenly turn tyrant, oppressing the weak and the defenseless. The brutality depicted by the late Mehmed Akif as:

"If toothless, one was devoured by his own brethren..." was a daily reality. The oppressed, trampled under the merciless feet of tyrants, fought an everyday battle for survival, with their screams of agony going unheard.

The Degrading Beliefs of the Age of Ignorance

The true faith had become corrupted. Some, supposing the Almighty too distant for them, believed that a divine force was embodied and had become manifest in natural objects like stones, rocks, fire, trees or mountains, which they considered sacred. There were some who worshipped the sun and the moon. By deeming them sacred and revering them, these people thought they could thereby reach Allah, glory unto Him.

Others were worshipping nonphysical beings like angels, *jinn* or the devil. If they worshipped and respected them well enough, they used to think, these beings could perhaps intercede on their behalf in Divine presence.

There were also idolaters who, on the one hand, claimed to believe in Allah, glory unto Him, while, on the other hand, ascribed partners to Him with various objects or things they wrought with their own hands. Despite their claim to be "the children of Ibrahim and Ismail –upon them peace-", they had long abandoned the belief in *tawhid*, the oneness of the Almighty, and were standing at a distant remove the *Hanif* path that the two prophets had bequeathed them. The idolaters would ascribe partners to Allah, glory unto Him, almost with anything one could think of.

And there was a further group in complete denial of the Almighty and the Hereafter, supposing everything to consist of this visible universe.

Harith, the foster father (Halimah's husband) of the Blessed Prophet -upon him blessings and peace-, had come to Mecca during the early stages of prophethood to pay a visit to the Prophet. The moment he arrived, he was met by idolaters, who said:

"Haven't you heard, Harith, what your son has been saying?"

"What has he been saying?" asked Harith.

"He has been claiming that Allah will resurrect mankind after death. He is also saying that Allah has two abodes called Heaven and Hell, where He will reward the obedient and punish the rebellious. These claims of his have disrupted our order and split out community!"

Harith eventually arrived next to the Blessed Prophet -upon him blessings and peace- and asked:

"What is this dispute between you and your tribesmen all about, dear? You have them complaining about you. They claim that you assure people that they are to be resurrected after death, where they will be bound for either Heaven or Hell."

"Yes, dear father", replied the Blessed Prophet -upon him blessings and peace-. "That is what I believe and say. If only I could hold you by the hand, right now, and explain how true those words are!"

Harith -Allah be well-pleased with him- later became Muslim and, as time went by, began reaping his share from the spiritual core of Islam. After his acceptance of Islam, he would say:

"How I wish he held me by the hand that day and explained to me the truth of his words and not let go until, with the permission of Allah, he ushered me to Paradise!" (Ibn Ishaq, Sirah, s. 218; Suhayli, Rawd'ul-Unuf, 284-285)

During the Age of Ignorance, people were sunk in many false beliefs. They were undergoing a virtual humanitarian tragedy, demeaning to what essentially defined them as human beings, their reason and conscience.

It was almost impossible to find a sound thought, a right idea. False ideas were running riot. And as a result, women were oppressed in society, mothers were banished and daughters were looked upon as bringing shame to the family.

One day, a Companion came to the Blessed Prophet -upon him blessings and peace- and said:

"We were an ignorant people, Messenger of Allah. We used to worship idols and bury our daughters alive. I had a little daughter who adored me. I remember...I used to call her and she would come running, overjoyed. I again called her one day and she came to me running. She began to walk by my side as I took her by the hand next to a nearby well that belonged to our family. Then grabbing her by the arm, I threw her into the well. The last words I heard from her, as she went crashing down the well, were her screams, 'daddy, daddy!'"

Upon hearing these chilling words, tears began flowing from the sparkling eyes of the Blessed Prophet -upon him blessings and peace-, the ocean of compassion. Another Companion present then began reproaching the person who had recounted this bitter experience. "You have no right to upset the Messenger of Allah!" he exclaimed.

"Leave him", interrupted the Blessed Prophet -upon him blessings and peace-. "He just wants to clear his chest about something that aggrieves him, something he feels is important." Then turning to that man, he said:

"Repeat what you just explained!" When the Companion retold his story, the Blessed Prophet -upon him blessings and peace- again broke down in tears, until his beard was left soaked. Turning to the man, once again, the Prophet of Allah -upon him blessings and peace- then stated:

"Allah has forgiven the sins committed in the Age of Ignorance of those who have become Muslims. Now, begin your life anew!" (Darimi, Muqaddimah, 1)

Humanity was clearly standing on the edge of a raging pit of fire. Spiritually, society had become a wreck, as individuals were on the brink of total ruin. Islam then arrived to save them from destruction and turned them into members of an exemplary society. Allah, glory unto Him, states:

"And hold fast by the covenant of Allah all together and be not disunited, and remember the favor of Allah on you when you were enemies, then He united your hearts so by His favor you became brethren; and you were on the brink of a pit of fire, then He saved you from it, thus does Allah make clear to you His communications that you may follow the right way." (Al-i Imran, 103)

Serving the Lord and His Creation were Ignored for Worldly Interests

Most authentic forms of worshipping were long forgotten and what remained was distorted. They had twisted beyond recognition many deeds of worship, like pilgrimage and sacrifice, to the tune of their false beliefs and vested interests. Claiming to give importance to worshipping, they were in fact promoting nothing but evil; though little did they know. They would, for instance, make pilgrims circumambulate naked, after which they would cover their clothing expenses just to flatter their own pride and self-conceit.

The only norm of social relations was power. Right and supremacy belonged to the powerful; the weak exercised no rights, whatsoever. There was not a trace left of peace and stability in society.

What Remained of Moral Qualities were Distorted from their Original Forms

It had gotten to a stage where the few moral qualities that somehow had managed to survive had become based solely on egoistical interests. They were either practiced in excess or in the bare minimum. Virtue had become a means for a boastful show of strength. They would waste in the name of generosity and commit the worst kind of murder thinkable: they would bury their daughters alive in the name of protecting their pride and honor.

True, a man of the Age of Ignorance was gallant; he always had his weapons close at hand. Courage was his trademark. But his courage was measured by the number of people he killed out of tribal hatred. His courage came from his ego and pride. Underlying his show of courage was an avid desire to prove both his and his tribe's supremacy. The ceaseless wars between tribes were hence eating them away, both physically and spiritually.

Abolishing the corrupt customs of Ignorance, Islam replaced them with the most beautiful and perfect principles of living. It restrained their unruly tempers with noble dispositions like patience, lenience and justice. Purifying their insensible and sentimental courage from egoism, it spiritualized it, directing it to nobler purposes. Islam taught them to use their courage in the way of superior ideals, like above all restoring justice and the Truth.

The man of the Age of Ignorance was generous and hospitable. But these virtues only served to attract praises for himself and his tribe. His grandest ambition was to be venerated, to hold a reputation among men with his nobility, generosity and courage, and awaken feelings of respect and awe in rivals. It was therefore not uncommon for one to slaughter six or seven sheep in one instant and have only their livers roasted for a feast while throwing out the rest of the meat, simply for the purpose of showing off.

While continuing to promote generosity and hospitality, Islam instilled them with a moral content. While acting generously, Muslims would steer clear from showing off and desire only the pleasure of Allah, glory unto Him. Consciousness of the Almighty being the True Owner of all things had, after all, been embedded in their hearts.

Accordingly, all riches belong to Allah, glory unto Him, and human beings only act as trustees.[1]

1 See, Al-i Imrân, 26; an-Nur, 33.

They have only limited authority over wealth and property and they come with certain responsibilities. Given as a trust by the Almighty, it is therefore necessary to put wealth to use in a manner approved and praised by the Almighty. It is vital to use wealth, which ultimately belongs to Allah, glory unto Him, in the service of His servants. One must thereby serve the Almighty by serving His created beings.

The Blessed Prophet -upon him blessings and peace- would say:

"The hand that gives is superior to the hand that receives."[2] But whilst giving, one was required to give only for the sake of the Almighty, remaining distant from pride, without any anticipation of worldly ends. The Holy Quran in fact advised and taught all human beings to say:

"We only feed you for Allah's sake; we desire from you neither reward nor thanks."[3]

Islam also prohibited wasting. So in stark contrast to the feast of the times of Ignorance, not even a single meat of a sheep slaughtered in the Age of Bliss would go to waste. Again, from feelings of generosity and selflessness, it was not uncommon for meat to pass around seven different families only to return to the same place from where it had been handed out in the first place.

---

2 Bukhari, Wasaya, 9; Muslim, Zakat, 97.

3 al-Insan, 9.

Desert life had led the man of Ignorance to a primitive notion of freedom. They would recognize no authority and rebel against any kind of authority that came. As a consequence, there was no central power. Social solidarity would scarcely go beyond the tribe. There was neither a system nor an institution of law that exercised a sanctioning power. Disagreements would either be referred to haphazardly chosen arbitrators or, more often than not, to the resolve of brute force.

Islam objected to an unlimited idea of freedom monopolized only by a small minority. The Quran's declaration that a slave with *iman* was more valuable than a nonbeliever[4] had thus left the idolaters furious. The fiercest protests against Islam therefore came from the ranks of the dominant class, the self-acclaimed free men. They informed the Blessed Prophet –upon him peace- that they would only be willing to negotiate with him on the condition he banished the slaves and the weak from around him; and that offer was unconditionally rejected by the Almighty.[5]

The morals of Islam aligned freedom to spirituality, basing the idea on moral grounds. It brought preventative measures to enable each person to limit his own freedom within his consciousness.

4 See, el-Baqara, 2٢1.
5 See, al-Kahf, 28.

The Holy Quran states:

"And certainly We created man, and We know what his mind suggests to him, and We are nearer to him than his jugular vein." (Qaf, 16)

"Do they not know that Allah knows what they keep secret and what they make known?" (al-Baqara, 77; al-Anam, 3)

A Muslim must therefore control not only his actions, but even his hidden tendencies. This essential thought brought about a profound and proportionately swift revolution in the spirit, perception of life and values of the man of Ignorance. He had now become subject to the heavenly authority and, at the same time, an external authority, as well as his own conscience. Given there was a dispute regarding a certain manner, he no longer resorted to brute force, but rather to the mediation of the verdict of Allah, glory unto Him and His Messenger. All Muslims had wholeheartedly embraced the need "to obey Allah, His Messenger and persons in charge from among them."[6]

Solidarity and mutual assistance during the Age of Ignorance would likewise never go beyond feelings of tribalism (*asabiyya*). The man of Ignorance was hardhearted and ruthless towards those he shared no

6 See, an-Nisa, 59.

blood ties with. The value of other beings was measured merely by the benefit they brought. There were simply no recognized limits in preventing others from usurping others' properties. They felt no unease whatsoever in even denying the wages of their workers.

Cleansing feelings of solidarity and mutual assistance from tribal bigotry, Islam reestablished them on the bases of love and compassion that were elevated by moral principles. It taught how to perceive all human beings gathered around the Islamic faith as brothers and to see them like the limbs of one body.[7]

The Blessed Prophet -upon him blessings and peace- one day said:

"Help your brother, even if he be the oppressed or the oppressor!" The Companions who heard it must have felt astonished to hear a motto of bygone tribal racism, seemingly spilling from the mouth of the Prophet of Allah -upon him blessings and peace- that one of them asked:

"If my brother is being oppressed, Messenger of Allah, I can help him. But how do I help him if he is the oppressor?"

The Blessed Prophet -upon him blessings and peace- then gave the magnificent answer below, attesting to the sensitivity of Islam:

7 See, Bukhari, Adab, 27.

"You keep him back from his oppression and prevent it from taking place. This, undoubtedly, is to help him." (Bukhari, Mazalim, 4; Ikrah, 6. Also see, Tirmidhi, Fitan, 68)

Islam thereby rectified their understanding of mutual assistance and returned it to its core. Assisting each other from then on would only be in goodness and piety; helping others in evil and hostility was now strictly forbidden.[8]

The Prophet's Great Miracle: The *Asr-u Saadah* Person

Qarafi (d. 684), among the most important figures in the methodology of Islamic jurisprudence, observes:

"Had the Prophet of Allah -upon him blessings and peace- not provided any miracles, the Companions he raised would have been more than sufficient to prove his prophethood."

So inspiring a potion were the Divine morals brought by the Blessed Prophet -upon him blessings and peace-, his outer training and the inner influence, that in rapid time they lifted an ignorant society previously in the wilderness, ignorant of even the basics of being human, to a level undreamed of, as 'the

8 See, al-Mâida, 2.

Companions', still envied by humankind even today. The ignorant and ruthless became cultivated, the wild became civilized and people with lowly and scandalous characters turned into righteous servants of the Almighty, who lived with the love and fear of Allah, glory unto Him, deeply set in their refined hearts.

Think of a man brutal and hardhearted enough to tear away a child from her grief-stricken mother and bury her alive...Merciless enough to inflict the most atrocious kinds of torture on slaves who he looked upon as nothing but a cheap personal item!

Finding guidance through Islam which imparted onto them a depth of consciousness, it was this previously ignorant and vulgar bunch of people, who were able to produce a civilization of virtues. At rock bottom in terms of humanly qualities during the Age of Ignorance, once they began implementing Islamic law and morals in their lives, they very able to climb the peaks of humanity.

The Age of Bliss Raised Exemplary Figures

From the society of Ignorance, which could not raise a single man of importance for centuries on end, there all of a sudden hailed numerous exemplary figures endowed with the highest moral qualities, thanks to the spiritual training and teaching of the Blessed Prophet -upon him blessings and peace-. And they carried the inspiration they received from the Quran and Sunnah to the four corners of the world, as flames of wisdom and knowledge. They showed no sign of weariness or fatigue. Hearts had become the receptacles of the love of Allah, glory unto Him, and they began perceiving the created with eye of the Creator, so to speak. Taking eternity under its wings, the Light that had descended onto the desert preached the Truth and justice to humankind entire.

The Muslims of the *Asr-u Saadah*, reared under the training of the Prophet of Allah -upon him blessings and peace-, the quintessential example for entire humanity, became members of a society of knowledge, wisdom, compassion and elegance who not only knew the Blessed Prophet -upon him blessings and peace- externally but also internally, with their hearts. That period was an age of deep contemplation, a time to gain an intimate knowledge of the Almighty and His Messenger.

The Companions placed *tawhid* in the center of their thoughts and ideals. They were successful in destroying worldly interests, selfish ambitions and the gods of desire that trickle into and wreak havoc in hearts. Life and wealth were demoted to being means rather than ends. Compassion grew deeper. Serving the Truth became a way of life. An enormous effort and sacrifice had the magnificent Islamic character put on display. Such that after traveling a month's distance just to confirm a *hadith* he already knew, a Companion would turn back after seeing that the man he had been seeking all along was tricking his horse with an empty fodder bag; an act of deception unbecoming of one to be trusted with the honorable task of confirming a *hadith* of the Prophet of Allah -upon him blessings and peace-.

Abu'l-Aliya, one of the great imams of the *Tabiun* generation, further explains this Islamic sensitivity in the following:

"Upon going next to someone with the intention of acquiring a *hadith*, we would observe the way he offered his ritual prayer. If we saw that he offered it nicely, we would think 'he must complete his other tasks in the same way' and then proceed to sit by his side and lend ear to him. Seeing him offer his ritual prayer in a sloppy manner, however, we would think 'this must be the case with all of his acts' and leave without giving him the time of the day." (Darimi, Muqaddimah, 38/429)

What did the Companions Receive from the Blessed Prophet -upon him blessings and peace-?

1. *Iniqas* or receiving reflections from the Blessed Prophet's -upon him blessings and peace- spiritual state, becoming one with him; an intensive flow of inspiration from the Prophet of Allah -upon him blessings and peace- to the Companions.

2. The learning of *aqrabiyya*; that is the teaching and practice of the way of gaining spiritual closeness to Allah, glory unto Him, and of recognizing Him in the heart.

A brand new understanding of Allah, glory unto Him, the universe and the self was imparted onto the Companions, akin to the Sun reflecting onto a tiny mirror. Becoming one with the spirituality of the Blessed Prophet -upon him blessings and peace- became their grandest ambition. In this way, the truth and the good became crystal clear in their lives in all their magnificence, as did the false with all its ugliness. Seeking the pleasure of the Almighty in every deed and each breath taken became a standard of life.

They were generous, compassionate, selfless and altruistic. Overcome with the love of worshipping, they lived only to serve the Truth.

The Companions underwent a test of faith in Mecca. In the end, they were able to remove all barriers that would have stood in the way of their *iman*. There came a time when they needed to sacrifice their riches just to show their power of *iman* and they did. There came a time when they were called onto sacrifice their lives and they did it just the same, without blinking their eyes. The faithful enthusiasm that swept them away in Mecca provided the spiritual groundwork for the unique civilization that was to be founded in Medina.

A Muslim society that exuded peace to the entire creation of the Almighty was thus founded. Deserts, scorched by the fire of mischief, found the peace they had been thirsting for. Even trees enjoyed a more peaceful environment; cutting green leaves for no good reason was prohibited. Islam's notion of justice saved not only human beings but also animals and plants from the grip of oppression, shining onto them the peace they had long been anticipating.

Islam Spread As Quickly As the Break of Dawn

The borders of the small Muslim city-state founded in Medina, made up of around four-hundred families, reached Iraq and Palestine, in only a matter of ten years. At the time of the passing away of the Noble Messenger -upon him blessings and peace-, the Companions had become strong enough to respond to the warmongering Byzantine and Persia. But their standards of living had little changed as compared to ten years before. They continued leading a life of abstinence. Excess consumption, greed, luxury and showing off were things unknown to them; they were filled with the constant awareness of the fact that 'awaiting their flesh, tomorrow, was but the grave.' They therefore always abstained from reserving the blessings of the world to themselves and using them up in excess. With the excitement and zest of *iman*, they instead used them as means for guiding humankind to its salvation. They molded their lives in the cast of seeking the pleasure of Allah, glory unto Him.

In fact, one of the main reasons behind the irrepressible dawning and spread of Islam, among the oppressed, outcast and exploited was the fact that the Companions displayed an excellent Muslim identity everywhere they went. As the elite students of the Blessed Prophet -upon him blessings and peace-, the Companions were an exceptional group of selfless, just and generous Muslims, who perceived the rest of creation with an eye of mercy, filled with the excitement of communicating the call of Islam.

At the core of friendship, they had placed Allah, glory unto Him, and His Messenger. A previously unlettered society thereby reached the peak of civilization; their hearts had become filled with the enthusiasm to become worthy persons in the sight of the Almighty and His Messenger.

Feelings Grew Deeper and More Spiritual

The Companions reached the furthermost point attainable by reason and spirit. Setting themselves free from the *nafsu'l-ammara* (the evil-commanding ego), they attained a perfected soul. They made a habit of questioning themselves over their conducts.

Restraining the desires of their egos and nourishing the abilities innate in their natural predisposition, they covered an enormous distance towards reaching Allah, glory unto Him. Previously in the wilderness, they thereby embodied angelic, delicate characters.

In the bottom end of the pit of ignorance and oppression, so to speak, they were eventually delivered to the shore of compassion and elegance by the spiritual reflections mirrored unto them of the Prophet's -upon him blessings and peace- inner world. They became exemplary figures in perceiving the world through the eyes of compassion.

The ruthless and callous man who once tore a little girl away from her frantic mother to bury her alive suddenly became a teary-eyed angel of mercy. His heart became a shelter for the weary and despondent members of society, a safe haven offering orphans, widows and the outcast a ray of hope and security.

The previously pitiless Omar -Allah be well-pleased with him- became a man of extraordinary sensitivity through Islam, to the extent that he would say, "I fear being called into account by Allah if a wolf was to snatch a lamb by the river Tigris!" (Ibn Abi Shaybah, Musannaf, VIII, 153)

Carrying a sack of flour on his back, he would look for the needy at night, with an ear out for their cries of desperation. The responsibility he felt over the welfare and happiness of the *ummah* became his greatest concern.

Another good example is Abdullah ibn Masud -Allah be well-pleased with him-. Upon sitting atop of Abu Jahl's chest as he lay sprawled on the battleground of Badr, the ingrained idolater threw him the following insult:

"You have sure climbed a high and steep hill you simple, miserable shepherd!" (Ibn Hisham, II, 277)

Ibn Masud -Allah be well-pleased with him- thus used to be a "simple shepherd" looked down upon by the rest of society. But receiving guidance and passing through training at the personal hands of the Blessed Prophet -upon him blessings and peace-, his heart became refined and grew as deep as the ocean, becoming a precinct of the manifestations of the Divine.

The great Kufa School, a major school of Islamic jurisprudence, was the very legacy of this celebrated Companion. Many Muslim jurists including Imam-i Azam Abu Hanifa, reputed to be the first scholar of Islamic law[9], hailed from this school. This circle of education raised men of such genius; such that figures like Solon and Hammurabi, who are universally renowned as great jurists, would not have been con-

9 Ali Haydar Efendi, *Dürerü'l-Hukkâm Şerhu Mecelleti'l-Ahkâm,* Istanbul 1330, p. 11.

sidered good enough to become apprentices to Abu Hanifa. Whichever discipline of Islamic science we may glance at, we will be sure to see the name of the great Abdullah ibn Masud -Allah be well-pleased with him- etched in the background.

They were living examples of the miracle that is the Holy Quran, pillars of prudence, wisdom and all values human.

The Functions of Reason and the Heart were in Harmony

The functions of reason and the heart, which ushered the Believers of the time to perfection, were used jointly, in harmony. By keeping their enthusiasm and love ever alive, they were able to grow their contemplation ever deeper.

They lived with the complete understanding that this life is nothing but a land of trial. Their hearts became accustomed to the flows of Divine Power and Majesty vibrant within the universe. They never showed any signs of tiredness in the long, arduous journeys they undertook to Central Asia, even to China, for the sake of enjoining the good and speaking against evil. Guided by the Quranic command forbidding him from throwing himself in danger with his very own hands,[10]

10 al-Baqara, 195.

Abu Ayyub al-Ansari -Allah be well-pleased with him-, joined military expedition of Istanbul, despite being well over eighty years of age at the time. In the end, he presented his mortal corpse to Istanbul as an endless memory and source of inspiration. His successors took the light of guidance as far as Andalus.

Uqbah ibn Nafi –May Allah have mercy on his soul-, of the *Tabiun* generation, was sent to Africa during the time of the Umayyads. He proceeded to capture Qayrawan and designated Zuhayr ibn Qays as administrator. "I have sold my soul to Allah and I shall fight those who deny Him until eternity", he then said to Zuhayr, instructing him his wishes should anything happen to him.

The all conquering Uqbah then continued his expeditions. The only thing stopping him was now the ocean. Steering his horse into the crashing waves, as he said:

يَا رَبِّ لَوْلَا هٰذَا الْبَحْرُ لَمَضَيْتُ فِى الْبِلَادِ

مُجَاهِدًا فِى سَبِيلِكَ

"If it was not for this ocean, My Lord, I would have continued to struggle in your way, along the towns lying in front of me!"[11] (Ibn'ul-Asir, al-Kamil fi't-Tarih, Beirut, 1385, IV, 105-106)

11 Uqbah ibn Nafi was a man whose prayers were often accepted. Completing his conquest of Northern Africa, he then came and stood in the middle of a rough terrain, where the town of Qayrawan is found today. Back then, it was a densely wooded

The first three centuries of the Ottomans who appeared in their wake and whose foundations were laid by a mere 400 warriors, was a virtual repeat of the age of the Companions.

Contemplation Became Profound

The society of Ignorance, previously living in pitch darkness, became the "truly knowledgeable" through the guidance of the Blessed Prophet -upon him blessings and peace-. The twilight made way for

---

area, seething with animals of prey. After praying to the Almighty, he said aloud the following, three times:

"Beasts of the valley! Allah-willing, we shall settle here. So better you leave!"

Witnessed shortly thereafter was a magnificent spectacle. Moving out of their burrows and nests underneath the trees, snakes and other predatory animals alike, began to move outside of the woods, many with their cubs on their backs. Uqbah then descended into the valley with his men and told them to "…settle here in the name of Allah".

Having witnessed this extraordinary scene, many of the local Berbers accepted Islam. (See, Dhahabi, *Tarihu'l-Islâm,* I, 601; Ibn Abdilbar, *Istiab,* I, 331; Ibn Kathîr, *al-Bidaya,* VIII, 45)

Proceeding forth in his conquests at the head of his army, Uqbah arrived camped at an arid place without water. So thirsty were his soldiers that they were on the brink of death, Uqbah thereupon offered a light *salat* and prayed. In the meantime, his horse was digging up the ground with its front hooves. There suddenly burst forth a spring of water from underneath it. Uqbah immediately called his soldiers, who digging the spot further, turned it into a well. They then drank to their hearts' content. That spring thereafter came to be known as *Mau'l-Faras,* literally 'Horse's Water.' (Ibn'ul-Asir, al-Kamil fi't-Tarih, IV, 106)

day, winter for spring. The quality of contemplation developed. People began reflecting on how the human being develops from a mere drop of water, trees from tiny seeds and like examples in nature. Their lives were aligned to the pleasure of Allah, glory unto Him. Compassion, kindness and the quality of conveying the truth enjoyed a splendor never before witnessed.

Communicating Islam became Their Most Enjoyable Activity

The Companions displayed the most beautiful Muslim character. Enduring all kinds of hardship, they sought the pleasure of the Almighty at every breath they took, in each moment of their lives. With such a spiritual blend, they avidly enjoined the good and the right and prevented others from evil and immorality. The most enjoyable and meaningful moments of life, for them, was when they would convey to others the message of *tawhid*.

The Blessed Prophet -upon him blessings and peace- could not meet women as often as he would meet men to communicate Islam. Guzayya -Allah be well-pleased with her-, a female who had entered the fold of Islam in the Meccan period was therefore providing much assistance in the spread of Islam. Secretly mixing in with Qurayshi women, she would extend to them the invitation to the Truth. She continued doing this until the idolaters of Mecca eventually found out. They seized her and sent her away to exile with a group of people from Daws, who were happening to be leaving Mecca at the time. They had her mounted, without a saddle, on a camel and depriving her of water, they then began torturing her until she entirely lost her sight, hearing and mind. Remorseful after having witnessed Guzayya's -Allah be well-pleased with her-- a unbelievable patience, courage and sincerity of *iman*, the group from Daws then ended up accepting Islam. (Ibn Saad, VIII, 155-157; Ibn Habbib, al-Muhabbar, p. 81-82, 92; Abu Nuaym, Hilya, II, 66-67; Ibn Hajar, al-Isabah, IV, 447)

Recovering thereafter, Guzayya -Allah be well-pleased with her- - made her Hegira to Medina just after the Prophet of Allah -upon him blessings and peace-. Some reports suggest she came to the Blessed Prophet -upon him blessings and peace- as an ambassador for the Abdulqays tribe.[12]

Once a woman taking some water to her tribe came across the Blessed Prophet -upon him blessings and peace- and witnessed one of his miracles. Upon her return, she explained her experience to her tribe, hearing which they accepted Islam in their entirety.[13]

12 Abu Khatib, *Asmau's-Sahâbah,* 142a, Istanbul University Library, A. 1101.

13 See, Bukharî, Tayammum, 6.

Neither were slave-women lagging behind free women in putting their efforts behind conveying Islam. In fact, a slave-girl from Isfahan, Persia, who had become Muslim before Salman the Persian -Allah be well-pleased with him-, guided him to the presence of the Blessed Prophet -upon him blessings and peace-.[14]

Another Companion, given three final minutes before his awaiting execution at the hands of idolaters, thanked the miserable men, adding, "That means I have another three minutes to invite you to Islam!"

In underlining the importance of *tabligh*, Abu Hurayrah -Allah be well-pleased with him- used to say:

"We used to hear the following spoken among the Companions: On the Day of Judgment a person will be grabbed by the scruff of the neck by another person who he never knew. Taken aback, he will ask:

'What do you want from me? I do not even know you!' The other person will then say, 'Despite seeing me on Earth committing evil deeds, you never used to warn me and hold me back!'

The man will then proceed to charge him in the Divine court of justice."[15]

---

14 Abu Nuaym al-Isfahanî, *Târîhu Isfahân,* I, 43; Ibnu'l-Asîr, *Usdu'l-Ghabah,,* VII, 25; Ibn Hajar, *al-Isabah,* IV, 233

15 Munziri, *at-Targhib we't-Tarhib,* Beirut 1417, III, 164/3506; R - dani, *Jam'u'l-Fawaid,* trns. Naim Erdoğan, Istanbul ts., V, 384.

They Held Fast to the Quran

Even the most difficult circumstances could not hold the Blessed Prophet -upon him blessings and peace- back from the Quran to the Companions. Abu Talha -Allah be well-pleased with him- one day saw the Blessed Prophet -upon him blessings and peace- teaching Quran to the students of the *Suffa*, standing. In order to keep his back, bent double from excruciating hunger, straight, he had tied a stone around his belly. (Abu Nuaym, Hilya, I, 342)

Thus the Companions' greatest concern was to understand the Book of the Almighty, to acquire its manifestations of wisdom and act in accordance. They had discovered the taste of life in repeating the Quran over and over, listening to it and implementing it in their lives.

In short, the Companions lived with the Quran and its content, devoting their entire lives to the Word of the Almighty. They showed a feat of self-sacrifice never before witnessed in history. They were subjected to worst kinds of oppression and torture but never did they compromise what they believed in. To implement the Holy Quran in their lives, they abandoned their entire wealth and properties, even their hometowns, and immigrated to Medina, for which they were more than ready to even let go of their lives.

The Companions were in a continuous endeavor to learn and put into practice each *ayah* of the Holy Quran. They never neglected the Quran, even during the most dangerous situations.

Abbad -Allah be well-pleased with him-, appointed by the Blessed Prophet -upon him blessings and peace- to keep guard over the Muslim forces had begun offering *salat*. The enemy, who had been on the lookout all along, began shooting arrows at him. Only after being shot with two or three arrows did Abbad -Allah be well-pleased with him- bow down to *ruqu* and then to *sajdah* and eventually complete his *salat*. He then informed his fellow guard Ammar -Allah be well-pleased with him-.

"Why did you not tell me when you had first been shot?" asked Ammar, somewhat astounded.

"I was reciting a *surah* of the Quran and I did not want to break my *salat* before completing it," replied Abbad. "But when the arrows hit me one after another I stopped reciting and bowed to *ruqu*. But by Allah, had there not been the fear of losing this spot whose protection the Messenger of Allah has ordered, I would have preferred death over cutting my recital of the chapter short." (Abu Dawud, Taharat, 78/198; Ahmad, III, 344; Bayhaki, Dalail, III, 459; Ibn Hisham, III, 219; Waqidi, I, 397)

The Companions led a life within the Quran's content. For them, each pillar of Islam was an insatiable taste. Each revealed *ayah* was like a feast from the heavens. All efforts were channeled to the aim of properly understanding and living the Quran and of setting the best example in regard. How great a portrait of virtue and testimony of an enthusiastic iman it is that, as *mihr* or dowry, a female Companion would only require her soon-to-be husband teach her the parts of the Quran he knew.[16]

The Companions took the enthusiastic effort of the Noble Prophet -upon him blessings and peace- towards the Quran as example and as a result the small town of Medina became filled with *huffaz* and scholars.

Factors that Directed the Companions to the Holy Quran

a. They were an unlettered society, never having come under the influence of a foreign culture. They were therefore able to focus all their intellectual and spiritual attention on the Quran. As a result, they produced a crowning culture; a culture which prevented injustice and oppression and acknowledged the right to life of every single creature on Earth.

A spiritual life of Islamic sensitivity is necessary for any human being. Only a superb spiritual

16 See, Bukhari, Nikah, 6, 32, 35; Fadailu'l-Quran, 21, 22; Muslim, Nikâh, 76.

blend could bring about beautiful cultural and artistic expressions and provide breadth and depth to contemplation. And only then can society raise men of the caliber of Mawlana Rumi, Sinan the Architect, Fuzuli the Poet and the likes.

b. Because the *ayat* of the Quran were gradually revealed, it made their memorization, practice and spiritual digestion of it easier. It provided the generation of Companions to undertake a gradual learning program.

c. That reciting the Quran during salat was made necessary meant that the Companions were continuously instilled with the Divine Word and that resulted in an increased bond. They were especially under the constant influence of *Surah* al-Fatiha, repeated at every *rakah* in a salat.

d. To make sure of that their judgments were correct and their deeds were accepted, they took lessons from the parables of the Holy Quran.

The Entire Humankind has Admired Them

Such was the *Asr-u Saadah*, the Age of Bliss that the Holy Quran generated in a very short amount of time. The entire world has since watched that unique generation behind admiring eyes.

If the entire psychologists, sociologists, pedagogues, social-anthropologists, philosophers and social engineers of the 21st century were to join forces, could they ever be able to train and raise just a handful of human beings of the blend of an entire society like that of the Companions?

The Quran and the Sunnah, which effectively brought about the *Asr-u Saadah*, still retain their liveliness, influence and applicability to this day. Societies that have clung onto Islam have always flourished while those who have abandoned it have perished. After examining Islam's principles of justice and freedom, La Fayette (d. 1834) has in fact felt obliged to pay homage to the Blessed Prophet –upon whom blessings and peace- in admiration:

"O you magnificent Arab! No matter how great your praises were they would not suffice; for you have discovered the very notion of justice!" (Kâmil Miras, *Tecrîd-i Sarîh Tercemesi,* IX, 289)

Islamic Morals are Practical, not Theoretical

Islam's aim is not to put forward an ordinary moral theory concerning various moral issues or to engage in a moral philosophy detached from everyday life and enter debates just for the sake of satisfying inquiring minds. Much rather, Islam's aim is to respond to the moral needs of human beings by offering practicable remedies and to provide them with an opportunity to become conscious of what personal mistakes they may have and, in time, to set themselves right. Islam desires the transferal of its moral principles to life, in the best and most dependable way possible. Not only does it aim for a morality that is "known" but also for one that is "practiced". Following straight after the first few *ayat* commanding the Noble Messenger -upon him blessings and peace- to "read" were those that ordered him to prohibit others from evil; and that fact alone deserves a thought.[17]

In contrast, the ideas put forth for the sake of establishing social peace and stability by philosophers whose minds never received the training of Divine Revelation, have more often than not never been able to go beyond the books they wrote, consigned the dusty shelves of libraries. As for those that have enjoyed some degree of practice, their lives have been short lived. Besides, these philosophers have been never able to practice what they preached in their own lives, let alone having a lasting influence on others. Hence, their ideas have always remained theories.

For instance, although Aristotle is known to have laid down certain principles of moral philosophy, because he was distant from Divine Revelation,

17 al-Alaq, 1-5; al-Muddaththir, 1-7.

we have never been able to witness a single person who has believed in his philosophy, practiced it and found happiness through it. Again, even Farabi's most important work *al-Madinatu'l-Fadila*, which contains his ideas of a perfect town and society, have never enjoyed the privilege of being practiced. These ideas were never able to beyond the lines of the book and have served no practical benefit apart from filling the appetite of hungry bookworms that feed on paper. Simply, they were not ideas preached through practice; nor were they ideas based in Divine Revelation fitting with the Will of the Almighty. "According to my own opinion", is what philosophers say, whereas prophets say "according to the command of the Almighty."

Briefly said, the Almighty again showed His eternal might by revealing to an unlettered Prophet the greatest knowledge of morality more than sufficient for the well-being and benefit of entire humankind. By allowing the Prophet -upon him blessings and peace- to put this great moral depth into practice through his quintessential character, the Almighty has furthermore shown just what His desired model of a human being is, for all eyes to see.

بِسْمِ اللهِ الرَّحْمٰنِ الرَّحِيمِ

وَمِنَ النَّاسِ مَنْ يَشْرِي نَفْسَهُ ابْتِغَاءَ
مَرْضَاتِ اللّٰهِ وَاللّٰهُ رَؤُفٌ بِالْعِبَادِ

And there is the type of man who gives his life to earn the pleasure of Allah: And Allah is full of kindness to (His) devotees.

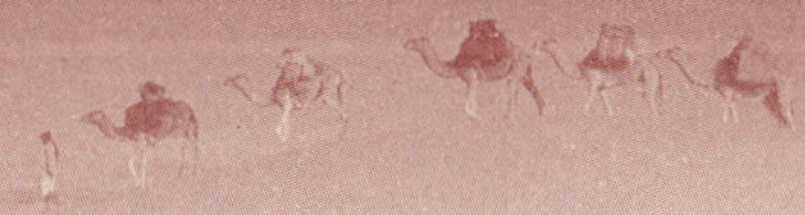

The Excitement of *Iman* in the *Asr-u Saadah* Society

The Excitement of *Iman* in the *Asr-u Saadah* Society

The Companions were in an enthusiastic effort to shape their lives according to their love and excitement of *iman*. At the bottom of this excitement of *iman* were the intense "spirituality and reflection" they had received from the Blessed Prophet -upon him blessings and peace-.

Indeed, the inner worlds of a society of Ignorance, which until then were devoid of the truth and moral values, became flooded with the spiritual downpours of mercy and abundance through the Blessed Prophet's -upon him blessings and peace- company. The inspiration, spirituality and reflected from the heart of the Blessed Prophet -upon him blessings and peace- onto theirs, brought about a collection of shining figures to light the way for humankind until the final hour. The unruly, hardhearted man of Ignorance, ruthless enough to bury his own daughter alive turned into a teary-eyed believer, a man of wisdom.

They Ran to Join the Circle of Islam

Young and old, the *Asr-u Saadah* society passionately ran to enter the ranks of the faithful. Abdullah ibn Zubayr -Allah be well-pleased with him- was the first child born after the Hegira. They immediately brought him next to the Prophet of Allah -upon him blessings and peace-. After chewing a small date in his mouth, the Prophet -upon him blessings and peace- placed it in the baby's mouth and stroking his head, prayed for him and named him Abdullah.

Once Abdullah -Allah be well-pleased with him- reached the age of eight, he was sent by his father to the Blessed Prophet -upon him blessings and peace- to pledge allegiance. Seeing the little Abdullah, the Messenger of Allah -upon him blessings and peace- smiled and accepted his pledge. (Muslim, Adab, 25)

Abdullah ibn Hisham -Allah be well-pleased with him- was still six during the conquest of Mecca when his mother Zaynab bint Humayd took him to the Blessed Prophet -upon him blessings and peace- and requested:

"Accept my son's pledge, Messenger of Allah, that he is a Muslim!"

"He is still young", replied the Blessed Prophet -upon him blessings and peace-, after which he stroked the young boy's head and prayed for him.

In his later years, Abdullah ibn Hisham -Allah be well-pleased with him- would go to the market and buy food items to trade. Upon seeing him, Ibn Omar and Ibn Zubayr -Allah be well-pleased with him- would straight away go next to him and ask him to "... make us partners in these items for the Messenger of Allah made a prayer of abundance for you!" Abdullah would comply with their requests. There were times when he would send them home with a camel load of profits. (Bukhari, Shirkah, 13)

Abu Kursafah -Allah be well-pleased with him-, too, had run to believe at a very tender age. He recounts his experiences below:

"As my mother, my aunt and I were returning home after having pledged our allegiances to the Messenger of Allah, I heard both of them say, 'We have never seen a man like him in our entire lives. We have never met another person with a more beautiful face, cleaner clothes and softer speech. It is as if it is light that spills from his mouth!" (Haythami, VIII, 279-280)

They Never Hesitated in Sacrificing Their Lives for Faith

Famous are the courageous feats of Sumayya and her husband Yasir -Allah be well-pleased with them-, who both sacrificed their lives just to protect their faith. Equally legendary is the courage of Ammar ibn Yasir, Bilal Habashi, Habbab ibn Arat, Suhayb ibn Sinan, Zinnira, Amir ibn Fuhayra, Abu Fukayha, Miqdad ibn Amr, Umm Ubays, Lubayna, Nahdiya and her daughter, all of whom were put through the most gruesome forms of torture, in spite of which they held fast to their *iman*. Even under unbearable persecution, the Companions were able to keep a strong hold on their beliefs, exerting an enormous effort just to make sure that this Divine blessings was passed on to future generations, safe and sound, even if it meant they had to give up all they had in the way.

During his days as Caliph, Omar -Allah be well-pleased with him- one day asked Habbab ibn Arat -Allah be well-pleased with him- to recount the torture he had been made to endure.

"Take a look at my back", Habbab -Allah be well-pleased with him- then said to him. After briefly inspecting his back, the chilled Omar -Allah be well-pleased with him- exclaimed, "I have never seen such a mutilated back in my life!"

"The idolaters used to light a fire", Habbab -Allah be well-pleased with him- then continued, "and make me lie on it without any clothes on my back. The fire would only be put out by the fat melting away from my back."

The idolaters would fasten onto Habbab's -Allah be well-pleased with him- back stones charred in by fire and the intensity of the pain would have the meat fall from his back, piece by piece. Still, he would not utter even a word of what the idolaters would demand him to say. (Ibn Asir, Usd'ul-Ghabah, II, 114-115)

Zayd ibn Dasina and Hubayb -Allah be well-pleased with them- who both fell captive to the idolaters were about to be tortured to death. Right before they breathed their last, they were both asked:

"Do you wish the Prophet was in your place right now in return for your life?" Both of them looked at the idolater posing the unfortunate question with pity and said:

"Let alone wishing the Prophet to be in my place right now and I with my family, I would not even want a thorn spiking his foot where he is!"

Petrified before the sight of an exceptional display of loyalty, Abu Sufyan, who was standing by, could not help but remark:

"How strange it is that I have never in my life seen another group of people than the Companions of Muhammad who love their leader more!" (Waqidi, I, 360-362; Ibn Saad, II, 56)

In the aftermath of the Battle of Uhud, Saffiya -Allah be well-pleased with her-- wanted to see the mutilated corpse of his brother Hamza -Allah be well-pleased with him-. With that intention in mind, she walked towards the corpses of the martyrs. Seemingly, the terrifying sight would have been too much for her to bear. His son Zubayr intercepted her and said:

"The Messenger of Allah advises you to return, dear mother!"

"Why?" she responded. "So I do not see my brother? I know he has been atrociously butchered. He has been subjected to this disaster in the way of Allah…and nothing short of that could have consoled us. Allah willing, I will keep patient and expect its rewards from Him!"

Zubayr -Allah be well-pleased with him- then turned back and recounted her mother's words to the Blessed Prophet -upon him blessings and peace-.

"In that case, allow her to see him", was his response.

Safiyya -Allah be well-pleased with her- said a heartfelt prayer by the side of his brother, who had attained to the honorable rank of the king of martyrs. (See, Ibn Hisham, III, 48; Ibn Hajar, al-Isabah, IV, 349)

Women, who in the Age of Ignorance would mourn for days on end, shredding their clothes and pulling their own hairs, over the smallest piece of bad news they received, had suddenly turned into pillars of composure, thanks to their unshakable belief in Allah, glory unto Him.

One of the most beautiful examples of this was provided by Kabsha bint Ubayd -Allah be well-pleased with her-, Saad ibn Muadh's -Allah be well-pleased with him- mother:

Having received heavy wounds at the Battle of Uhud, the Messenger of Allah -upon him blessings and peace- was returning to Medina on horseback, with Saad ibn Muadh -Allah be well-pleased with him- holding its reins, when Kabsha bint Ubayd -Allah be well-pleased with her- began approaching them.

"This is my mother, Messenger of Allah", said Saad -Allah be well-pleased with him-.

"Peace to her", replied the Blessed Prophet -upon him blessings and peace-.

Drawing closer to the Prophet -upon him blessings and peace- and gazing at his face, she then said, "May my parents be ransomed for you, Messenger of Allah. All troubles mean nothing to me, now that I have seen you safe and sound!"

After giving his condolences to her over her son Amr ibn Muadh -Allah be well-pleased with him-, martyred on the battlefield of Uhud, the Blessed Prophet -upon him blessings and peace- added, "I give you and your entire household glad tidings.

Every single martyred member of your tribe (twelve all up) has now come together in Paradise. They have also been given permission to intercede on behalf of their families!"

"We are satisfied, Messenger of Allah. Who would shed tears over them after now?" she responded before pleading, "Please pray for those of us who are left behind, too!"

So the Noble Messenger -upon him blessings and peace- prayed:

"Allah…Rid their hearts of sorrow and give them their rewards over their troubles! And protect those who have been left behind in the best way!"

The Messenger of Allah -upon him blessings and peace- then continued on his way. The Companions were following in his wake. Their love for the Prophet -upon him blessings and peace- prevented them from going home; they much preferred to remain by his side. Sensing the situation, the Blessed Prophet -upon him blessings and peace-, addressing Saad -Allah be well-pleased with him-, said:

"There are plenty of people from your tribe who have been heavily wounded. On the Day of Judgment, they shall all emerge with blood flowing from their wounds. Its color will be that of blood but will smell of musk. Tell them to return home and treat their wounds. Let nobody follow us from hereon. Tell them that this is an imperative order!"

"It is the Messenger of Allah's -upon him blessings and peace- imperative command that no wounded person from the Banu Ashal tribe shall follow us from hereon!" Saad -Allah be well-pleased with him- called out. The wounded warriors, thirty all up, had no other choice than to return unwillingly. They spent the entire night dressing their wounds around fires which remained lit until morning. (Waqidi, I, 315-316; Diyarbakri, I, 444)

Another female Companion who put on a display of fortitude almost beyond human capacity was Sumayra -Allah be well-pleased with her-.

On the Day of Uhud, Medina trembled with the news that the Prophet -upon him blessings and peace- had been martyred. Panic broke loose as screams reached the Heavens. Such that despite being told that her husband, two sons, father and brother had been martyred on the battlefield, Sumayra -Allah be well-pleased with her-, an *Ansari* woman, remained indifferent, concerned only to be comforted with the news of the Blessed Prophet's -upon him blessings and peace- wellbeing, as she continuously kept on asking:

"Is *he* all right?"

She eventually got the reply she was hoping for, from the incoming Companions:

"Yes. *Alhamdulillah* he is alive and well!"

But Sumayra -Allah be well-pleased with her- was little contented.

"Show him to me so my heart rests at ease", she implored. When they did, she rushed to the Prophet of Allah -upon him blessings and peace-, and holding him by the edge of his shirt, exclaimed:

"May my parents be sacrificed for you, Messenger of Allah… I have nothing to worry about so long as you're alive!" (Waqidi, I, 292; Haythami, VI, 115)

They Struggled and Migrated Just to Protect their Faith

To protect their *iman* from the oppression of the Meccan idolaters, the Companions migrated to distant lands, leaving behind their hometowns, families and wealth. As a testimony of their strength of faith, Allah, glory unto Him, states in the Holy Quran:

"Those who believed and left their homes and strove for the cause of Allah, and those who took them in and helped them - these are the believers in truth. For them is pardon, and bountiful provision." (al-Anfal, 74)

The speech of Jafar Tayyar -Allah be well-pleased with him-, designated by the Prophet -upon him blessings and peace- as the head of the first envoy of immigrants to Abyssinia, in the presence of the Negus, provides a wonderful idea of how an ignorant people were transformed into exemplary figures and the excitement that remained with them thereafter:

"Your majesty! We were an ignorant bunch. We used to worship idols made of wood thinking they are gods. We used to eat carrion and bury our daughters alive. We were gamblers, indulgers in usury. We fornicated and saw no harm in seeing a woman engage in relations with numerous men. Neither did we know anything of the rights of our relatives, nor did we recognize the rights of neighbors. The strong used to oppress the weak, while the rich lived off the poor. We knew nothing of justice!

Then Allah the Almighty showed mercy on us and willed our recovery, and sent a Prophet from among us, from a noble line and a virtuous tribe. We had already known him as the Trusted. He called us to the oneness of Allah. He taught us how to worship Him. He saved us from the idols of our ancestors. He warded off all evil from us. He banned the shedding of blood, usury, lying and the misuse of orphans' properties. He constantly taught us what is good. He advised us righteousness, to keep our word, to treat neighbors and relatives with kindness and to protect the honor of women and the lives of our daughters. He saved us from savagery and taught us how to be humane. So we believed him and now we walk on his path.

For that very reason we have earned the hostility of the Quraysh. We were tortured. When the suffering became unbearable, and since we did not want to leave our religion either, we asked permission of our Prophet -upon him blessings and peace-, and favoring you over other kings we came to your land. We assumed we would not be oppressed here and so we took shelter in your protection." (Ahmed, I, 202-203, V, 290-291; Haythami, VI, 25-27; Ibn Hisham, I, 358-359)

The last convoy of immigrants to Abyssinia returned, by sea, to the Blessed Prophet -upon him blessings and peace- during the conquest of Khaybar. Asma bint Umays -Allah be well-pleased with her- was also among them. One day, she visited Hafsa -Allah be well-pleased with her-, the wife of the Blessed Prophet -upon him blessings and peace-, and as she was there, Hafsa's father Omar -Allah be well-pleased with him- stepped inside. Unable to recognize Asma, he asked who she was. When Hafsa -Allah be well-pleased with her- revealed her identity, Omar -Allah be well-pleased with him- asked, lightheartedly:

"Is that the Asma from Abyssinia…the one who took part in the sea voyage?"

"Yes", replied Asma -Allah be well-pleased with her-.

"We have surpassed you in terms of Hegira", then said Omar -Allah be well-pleased with him-. "We therefore have more right to be closer to the Messenger of Allah!"

Saddened by his words, Asma responded, "By Allah, you are wrong to think that, Omar! All this time, you were with the Messenger of Allah…he fed your hungry and taught your ignorant. But we were in a land distant, in Abyssinia, among foreign people, living in exile. And it was all in the name of Allah and His Messenger. I promise by Allah that I will not eat or drink anything until I tell the Messenger of Allah what you just told me. We had to endure a lot of suffering and intimidation there. But I will sure inform the Messenger of Allah of this and learn the insight into the matter. I will tell him just the way it is, without lying or adding anything of my own!"

The moment the Blessed Prophet -upon him blessings and peace- arrived, Asma -Allah be well-pleased with her- notified him of Omar's -Allah be well-pleased with him- words. After receiving Omar's -Allah be well-pleased with him- confirmation, the Messenger of Allah -upon him blessings and peace- said:

"He has no greater right by me than you. He and his friends have only one Hegira while you, the sea voyagers, have two!"

Asma -Allah be well-pleased with her- says:

"Immediately afterwards, Abu Musa al-Ashari and the other Companions aboard the ship from Abyssinia came to me in groups and had me retell the words of the Messenger of Allah -upon him blessings and peace-. It was as if there was nothing else on Earth that made them happier and gave them greater hope. Abu Musa al-Ashari -Allah be well-pleased with him- had me repeat the incident over and over again, receiving an insatiable delight each time I recounted him the glad tidings given to the immigrants of Abyssinia." (Bukhari, Maghazi, 36; Muslim, Fadail'us-Sahaba, 169)

واعبد ربك حتى يأتيك اليقين

صدق الله العظيم

١٤٠٩

The Thrill of Worshipping in the Age of Bliss

The Thrill of Worshipping in the Age of Bliss

For the Companions, times of worshipping were moments of closeness and intimacy with Allah, glory unto Him. These times therefore provided important and unique opportunities to find inner peace. They would offer each deed of worship with the excitement that came with the privilege of having been subjected to Divine commands, perceiving it an honor and an enormous blessing just to be gifted with the ability to fulfill each deed of worship.

They Took Care to Be with *Wudu* at All Times

The Muslims of the Age of Bliss were careful to be with *wudu* at all times and refresh it with each approaching *salat*. The Blessed Prophet -upon him blessings and peace- one day called Bilal Habashi -Allah be well-pleased with him- next to him and asked:

"Which deed was it you did that made you enter Paradise before me? Whenever I enter Paradise in my dreams I hear your shoes tapping in front of me. Last night I once again entered Paradise and heard the tapping of your shoes in front of me once again…"

"I make sure to offer two *rakat* of salat every time I hear the *adhan*, Messenger of Allah! When I break my *wudu*, I quickly refresh it and think that I owe Allah another two *rakat*," explained Bilal -Allah be well-pleased with him-.

"Owing to those two, then", the Messenger of Allah -upon him blessings and peace- stated. (Tirmidhi, Manaqib, 17/3689; Ahmed, V, 354)

Abu Ghutayf al-Huzali explains:

"I listened to Abdullah ibn Omar in the Masjid as he spoke to us seated on the floor. When it was the time for *zuhr* salat, he got up from his spot, took *wudu* and offered salat. Once the time for *asr* salat came, he again got up from his spot, took another *wudu* despite retaining his previous *wudu* and offered salat. When it was time for *maghrib* salat, he again refreshed his *wudu* and offered the salat. Afterwards, he returned to his spot.

'May Allah render you among the righteous', I said to him. 'Is it obligatory (*fard*) or voluntary (*sunnah*) to refresh the *wudu* for each salat?'

'Were you observing me all this time?' he asked.

'Yes', I answered.

'No, it is not obligatory', he then explained. 'When I took *wudu* for fajr salat, I could have offered every salat thereafter with the same *wudu*, so long as I did not break it; if it were not for these words I heard from the Messenger of Allah -upon him blessings and peace-:

'Whosoever takes *wudu* over another *wudu* is given ten rewards.'

'So it is those rewards I am after', he said. (Ibn Majah, Taharat, 73)

The Companions used to do justice to their *wudu*, taking it as thoroughly as it can be. Abu Hazim of the *Tabiun* generation once saw Abu Hurayrah -Allah be well-pleased with him- wash his arms up to his armpits whilst taking *wudu*.

"What sort of a *wudu* is that, Abu Hurayrah?" he asked.

"Were you here? I would not have taken *wudu* in that manner had I known you were. But I heard the Messenger of Allah -upon him blessings and peace- once say, 'The light of a believer on the Day of Judgment will reach to the furthermost point reached by his *wudu* water.'" (Muslim, Taharah, 40)

The Blessed Prophet -upon him blessings and peace- one day went to the graveyard and said:

"Greetings to you, dwellers of the land of believers! Allah willing, we will one day unite! How I wished to have seen my brothers!"

"Are we not your brothers?" instantly wondered the Companions.

"You are my companions", replied the Blessed Prophet -upon him blessings and peace-. "Our brothers are those who are not yet born into this world."

"How will you recognize them, Messenger of Allah -upon him blessings and peace-?" they then asked.

"Think of someone who has a horse that has a white forehead and hooves. Will he not be able to recognize his horse in a herd of pitch black horses?"

"Of course he would!"

The Noble Prophet -upon him blessings and peace- thereupon said, "There...(On the Day of Judgment) Your brothers will come with their faces, hands and feet lit from the light of *wudu*. I will arrive at the head of my pool and wait for them, to treat them. Beware! Certain people will be banished from my pool just as a foreign camel is banished from the herd. I will call out to them for them to come. But it will be said to me, 'They changed their ways after you!'

Thereupon I will say, 'Then let them remain distant, distant!'" (Muslim, Taharah, 39; Fadail, 26; Nasai, Taharah, 110/150; Ibn Majah, Zuhd, 36; Muwattaa, Taharah, 28; Ahmed, II, 300, 408)

Salat was the Light of Their Eyes

The believers of *Asr-u Saadah* used to offer their salat with the feeling and excitement of reunion with Allah, glory unto Him. They would perform it with an enormous longing and concentration, as one would when offering his very final salat in life.[18]

Saad ibn Abi Waqqas -Allah be well-pleased with him- recounts:

"There were two brothers. One of them had died forty days before the other. People began speaking of the virtues of the one who had passed away before the other, in the presence of the Messenger of Allah -upon him blessings and peace-.

'Wasn't the other brother a Muslim, too?' then asked the Messenger of Allah -upon him blessings and peace-.

'Yes, Messenger of Allah. He sure was', they replied. The Messenger of Allah -upon him blessings and peace- then said:

18 See, Ibn Majah, Zuhd, 15; Ahmed, V, 412.

'How are you to know the ranks granted to him by the salats he offered? Salat is like a luscious and sweet river that flows in front of a person's door, in which he bathes five times a day. What do you say... will that leave anything of dirt on that person? You could not imagine the ranks salat elevates a person to!" (Muwattaa, Qasr'us-Salat, 91)

Abu Talha -Allah be well-pleased with him- was once offering salat under the shade in his garden. A bird known as *dubsi* began flapping its wings in a bid to fly outside of the garden, fluttering to and fro to find a spot from which to exit. Abu Talha was taken in by the beauty of the sight and momentarily fixed his eyes on the bird. He then came around to himself and returned to his salat but he could not remember at exactly which stage he was at. "My possessions have caused me trouble and have caused a lapse in my concentration", he thought, referring to his garden, as he went to the Blessed Prophet -upon him blessings and peace-. There, he informed him of what had happened and said:

"I hereby hand this garden over as charity in the way of Allah. You can use it as you wish, Messenger of Allah, and give it to who you see fit." (Muwattaa, Salat, 69)

During his time as caliph, Omar -Allah be well-pleased with him- is reported to have written the following to his governors:

"As far as I am concerned, you most important duty is salat. Whosoever offers it nicely, observing its guidelines and designated times, will have protected his religion. Whosoever neglects it will neglect the other commands of religion even more." (Muwattaa, Wuqut'us-Salat, 6)

The following is from Miswar ibn Mahramah -Allah be well-pleased with him-:

"I visited Omar ibn Khattab -Allah be well-pleased with him- after he was daggered. They had put a blanket over him as he lay unconscious.

'How is he?' I asked those attending to him.

'As you can see', they said.

'Call him to salat', I suggested, 'for there is nothing other than salat that could frighten him to awake!'

They thereupon announced, 'Caliph…It is time for salat!'

Omar -Allah be well-pleased with him- instantly got up from his bed, remarking, 'True…and by Allah he who abandons salat has no share of Islam!'" (Haythami, I, 295. Also see, Muwattaa, Taharat, 51; Ibn Saad, III, 35)

Ali -Allah be well-pleased with him- also said to one of his officials, "Everything depends on your salat!"[19]

19 Abdülaziz Çaviş, *Anglikan Kilisesine Cevap*, p. 96.

Alaa ibn Abdurrahman recounts the following incident:

"It was afternoon, when on one occasion we paid a visit to Anas ibn Malik. When we arrived, Anas instantly stood and offered his *asr* salat. We told him he had offered the salat too early. Then in explaining his reason for doing so, he said:

'I once heard the Messenger of Allah -upon him blessings and peace- say, "That is the salat of hypocrites! That is the salat of hypocrites! That is the salat of hypocrites! (…the salat of those carrying signs of hypocrisy in their hearts). They sit and sit right until the sun turns yellow and begins to set and take its place right between the two horns of the devil, and quickly get down and get back up four times, like a bird collecting seed, and very little do they remember Allah in their salat." (Muwattaa, Quran, 46; Muslim, Masajid, 195)

As a result of the warnings of the Blessed Prophet -upon him blessings and peace-, the Companions were very diligent in observing the proper measure of each action in the salat. One day, Huzayfa -Allah be well-pleased with him- saw a person offering salat in the Masjid, yet without doing his *ruku*s and the *sajdah*s properly. Afterwards, Huzayfa -Allah be well-pleased with him- asked him, 'How many years have you been doing it like this?'

'Forty years', replied the man.

'Well, that means you have not been offering salat for forty years. If you die while still offering your salat this way, you will have died upon something other than the predisposition (*fitra*) on which Muhammad -upon him blessings and peace- was created." He then proceeded to show the man the proper way of offering salat, adding:

'A person may be excused for offering light salat, only on the condition that his does his *ruku*s and *sajdah*s properly!" (Ahmed, V, 384; Bukhari, Adhan, 119, 132; Salat, 26)

They Never Remained Back from *Jamaah*

The most important hallmark of the *Asr-u Saadah* society was the replacement of tribalism with the consciousness of religious brotherhood and the founding of a magnificent social unity and solidarity. And the clearest manifestation of this social unity in daily life was the salats offered in congregation or *jamaah*.

As an imam well acquainted with his *jamaah*, the Blessed Prophet -upon him blessings and peace- used to instantly realize when someone was missing. He would ask, "Has so and so come to salat?" "Where is your friend so and so?" Given the person missing was ill, he would pay him a visit with his Companions. If the person had a problem, he would see to it either by going there or calling the person next to him.

In encouraging Muslims to attend *jamaah*, the Blessed Prophet -upon him blessings and peace- would say:

"If you see someone who has made a habit of attending mosques, testify to his faith; for Allah the Almighty has said:

'Only he shall visit the mosques of Allah who believes in Allah and the Hereafter...' (at-Tawba, 18)" (Ibn Majah, Masajid, 19)

Thus, frequenting the congregation is a sign of *iman*, as it is classed as keeping mosques alive.

Abdullah ibn Masud -Allah be well-pleased with him- says:

"By Allah, I never witnessed anyone of us lag behind the *jamaah* apart from those who were exposed as hypocrites. I promise by Allah that an ill man would be brought to the mosque despite dragging his feet between two men carrying him on either side and would be placed in a row with their support." (Muslim, Masajid, 256-257)

There were two Muslims during the time of the Blessed Prophet -upon him blessings and peace-. One of them was a merchant, while the other a blacksmith specializing in making swords. Upon hearing the *adhan*, the merchant would instantly put aside his scale or leave it on the ground as it is and rush to the *Masjid*.

Likewise, the blacksmith would leave his hammer on his anvil or throw it behind his back given he was about the bang it on the sword in front of him and immediately make his way to the *Masjid*. In praise of them and Muslims alike, the Almighty revealed the following:

"Men whom neither trade nor selling diverts from the remembrance of Allah and the keeping up of prayer and the giving of poor-rate; they fear a day in which the hearts and eyes shall turn about." (an-Nur, 37) (Qurtubi, XII, 184)

While in the bazaar, Ibn Masud -Allah be well-pleased with him- one day saw a group of people running to the mosque upon hearing the *adhan*. He thereupon remarked, "These are the people praised by Allah in *an-Nur* (in the ayah just mentioned)". (Haythami, VII, 83)

They Used to Give Alms with Pleasure

The *Asr-u Saadah* society used to place great importance on alms or *zakat*, as the Almighty was adamantly enjoining alms, along with salat, on numerous occasions in the Quran. They would give their alms and charity as if they were handing directly to the hand of the Almighty, experiencing grand emotions and excitement while doing so.

With a sense of urgency in offering a good deed, Abbas -Allah be well-pleased with him-, the Blessed Prophet's -upon him blessings and peace- uncle, once asked whether he could give his alms before the required year had passed. The Blessed Prophet -upon him blessings and peace- gave him permission. (Abu Dawud, Zakat, 22/1624; Tirmidhi, Zakat, 37/678; Ibn Majah, Zakat, 7; Ahmed, I, 104; Darimi, Zakat, 12)

A woman, who was a relative of the Blessed Prophet -upon him blessings and peace-, once visited him with her daughter by her side. Her daughter was wearing two bracelets, which were rather thick, on her wrists.

"Do you give their alms?" the Blessed Prophet -upon him blessings and peace- asked the woman, referring to the bracelets.

"No", she replied.

"Would you like it if Allah made you wear two bracelets of fire in their place?" the Prophet -upon him blessings and peace- then asked.[20]

---

20 There is dispute among Muslim scholars concerning the *zakat* of jewelry. Offering it is, nonetheless, of greater discretion.

The woman then immediately removed them from her daughter's wrists and handed them over, saying, "These now belong to Allah and His Messenger. Do with them as you wish!" (Abu Dawud, Zakat, 4/1563)

A thirteen man envoy of the Banu Tujib tribe had arrived next to the Noble Messenger -upon him blessings and peace- with their alms to pay. The Prophet -upon him blessings and peace- was fond of sensitivity towards alms and after warmly welcoming them, told Bilal Habashi -Allah be well-pleased with him- to host them in the best way possible.

"We have brought to you, Messenger of Allah, what is Allah's due in our wealth!" they said.

"Take them back with you and distribute it among your poor", said the Blessed Prophet -upon him blessings and peace-.

"But we have only brought with us what was left over from our poor", they explained.

Abu Bakr -Allah be well-pleased with him- then praised them, commenting, "Surely there is no other envoy among other Arabs like these men of Tujib, Messenger of Allah!"

"Guidance is in the hands of Allah", then stated the Noble Prophet -upon him blessings and peace-. "Allah opens to *iman* the hearts of whom He wishes for the best."

The envoy of Banu Tajib asked the Blessed Prophet -upon him blessings and peace- certain questions about the Quran and Sunnah. Their answers were written down and handed to them. Their enthusiasm increased the Prophet's -upon him blessings and peace- interest towards them. After staying a few days, the envoy expressed their desire to return. When asked as to why they were in such a hurry, they said:

"We want to return to our people as soon as possible so we can teach them what we saw and learnt of the Messenger of Allah!" They saw the Prophet of Allah -upon him blessings and peace- one last time and bode him farewell. The Prophet -upon him blessings and peace- sent Bilal Habashi -Allah be well-pleased with him- with them and granted them more gifts than any other envoy. (Ibn Saad, I, 323; Ibn Qayyim, III, 650-651)

Ibn Abbas -Allah be well-pleased with him- recounts:

"The Messenger of Allah -upon him blessings and peace- led a two *rakah* salat one a day of *eid*. After giving a sermon to the males, he drew closer towards where the women were, as they could not hear him properly. With him was Bilal -Allah be well-pleased with him-. He then preached them, too, encouraging them to give charity. Thereupon, the women began to throw their bracelets, gold and silver necklaces and rings on Bilal's stretched out shirt." (See, Bukhari, Zakat, 21, 33)

Drawing attention to how neglect in fulfilling financial deeds of worship ends up becoming a reason for tragic remorse, Ibn Abbas -Allah be well-pleased with him- used to warn people with the following words:

"Whosoever does not perform his pilgrimage or offer his alms despite having the threshold amount of wealth, will sincerely wish to return to life during his final breath". He would then recite the below *ayah*:

"O you who believe! let not your wealth, or your children, divert you from the remembrance of Allah; and whoever does that, these are the losers. And spend out of what We have given you before death comes to one of you, so that he should say: My Lord! Why did You not respite me to a near term, so that I should have given alms and been of the doers of good deeds? And Allah does not respite a soul when its appointed term has come, and Allah is Aware of what you do." (al-Munafiqun, 9-11) (Tirmidhi, Tafsir, 63/3316)

The people of the Age of Bliss were thoroughly sensitive with regard to the portion of their wealth they were obliged to safeguard and forward to the needy.

Ahnaf ibn Qays -Allah be well-pleased with him- one day arrived next to Caliph Omar -Allah be well-pleased with him-, as the head of the envoy from Iraq. It was an extremely hot day. Wearing an apron, Omar -Allah be well-pleased with him- was oiling a camel allocated for alms and tending to it. Seeing them, he said:

"Change your clothes, Ahnaf…and come and help me; for this is a *zakat* camel. And the poor, widowers and orphans are entitled to it."

One of them then said, "May Allah have mercy on you, Caliph! Couldn't you instead get one of your slaves to do it?"

To that, Omar -Allah be well-pleased with him- gave the wonderful response below:

"Who is a better slave than Omar and Ahnaf? Since it is I who has taken the responsibility of all Muslims on my shoulders, it is me who is the slave of all Muslims! Just as it is necessary for a slave to be sincere towards his master and fulfill all his responsibilities, I, too, must conduct myself in the same way towards Muslims." (Ali al-Muttaqi, V, 761/14307)

There are also reports that Omar -Allah be well-pleased with him- once chased a runaway *zakat* camel until he virtually ran out breath and responded in a similar tone to those advising him to instead get one of his servants to chase the camel down.

An indication of the sensitivity shown by the early Muslims towards alms is the case of Caliph Omar ibn Abdulaziz. The official alms distributor he sent to Africa returned without giving away a single grain of alms, for the simple reason that he could not find a single person in need. The Caliph then used the alms to purchase and set free an enormous amount of slaves.[21]

Charitableness was the Focal Point of their Lives

The *Asr-u Saadah* society knew very well that giving charity in the way of Allah, glory unto Him, would shield a person from many dangers and troubles, as well as helping him attain to the love of the Almighty. After all, the Quran had declared:

"And spend[22] in the way of Allah and cast not yourselves to perdition with your own hands, and do good (to others); surely Allah loves the doers of good." (al-Baqara, 195)

Umm Bujayd -Allah be well-pleased with her-, a female Companion, had once come to the Blessed Prophet -upon him blessings and peace-, lamenting:

"The blessings of Allah unto you, Messenger of Allah. Many a time, a needy person comes and stands in front of my door, yet I am not able to find anything to give!"

---

21 Said Ramadan al-Buti, *Fiqhu's-Sirah,* Beirut 1980, p. 434.

22 Infaq, translated as 'spend', not only comprises alms but also e - ery good deed offered with a genuine intent. (See, the "İnfak" entry, *Diyânet İslâm Ansiklopedisi,* XXII, 289)

"Even if you cannot find anything else than a burnt sheep's nail" said the Blessed Prophet -upon him blessings and peace-, "give it to the poor and do not let him return empty handed." (Abu Dawud, Zakat, 33/1667; Tirmidhi, Zakat, 29/665; Nasai, Zakat, 70/2566; Ahmed, VI, 383)

Even if a Muslim does not have anything to give, he should at least console the needy with a few kind words. In a situation like this, the Almighty advises to say قَوْلًا مَيْسُورًا: that is sweet and gentle words that will impart a feeling of peace and joy.

In underlining the abundance that comes with giving, Abu Masud al-Ansari -Allah be well-pleased with him- says:

"After the Messenger of Allah -upon him blessings and peace- commanded us to give charity, some began going to the bazaar to carry loads on their backs in return for a payment of a *mudd*,[23] which they would then give away in charity. Some of those people today have as many as a hundred-thousand dinars." (Bukhari, Zakat, 10)

"Each person will be shaded by the charities he gave until the verdict is passed (in the Hereafter)", says the Blessed Prophet -upon him blessings and peace-.

Abu'l-Khayr, one of the transmitters of the above *hadith*, used to make sure he donated something

23 A *mudd* is a unit of weight which roughly equates to 687 grams.

every day, even if it meant it was in the form of a loaf of bread, an onion or little things like that. (Ahmed, IV, 147-8; Haythami, III, 110)

Omar -Allah be well-pleased with him- recounts:

“The Messenger of Allah -upon him blessings and peace- had ordered us to donate. I possessed a reasonable amount of wealth at the time, too. ‘If there was ever a time I could outdo Abu Bakr’, I thought to myself, ‘it is today’. So I brought half of my entire wealth and handed it over to the Messenger of Allah -upon him blessings and peace-.

‘What have you left for your family’, asked the Messenger of Allah -upon him blessings and peace-.

‘Around the same amount as what I have brought’, I replied.

But then Abu Bakr -Allah be well-pleased with him- turned up with his entire wealth.

‘What have you left for your wife and kids?’ asked the Messenger of Allah -upon him blessings and peace-.

‘I have left Allah and His Messenger’, he replied.

It was right there and then that I realized I could not outdo him in anything!” (Tirmidhi, Manaqib, 16/3675)

According to Abdurrahman ibn Abu Amra, one night her mother declared she would free a slave come morning, only to die the same night. So he later went to Qasim ibn Muhammad, asking him whether he could set a slave free on behalf of her mother.

Qasim said, "Saad ibn Ubadah -Allah be well-pleased with him- once asked the Messenger of Allah -upon him blessings and peace- whether her deceased mother would receive any benefit if he freed a slave on behalf of her. 'Yes', was his reply.'" (Muwattaa, Itq, 13)

Aisha -Allah be well-pleased with her- reports that a man once came to the Blessed Prophet -upon him blessings and peace- and said, "My mother suddenly passed away. I am sure that if she could have spoken, she would have certainly given charity. Could I give charity on her behalf?"

"Yes", assured the Noble Messenger -upon him blessings and peace-. "Do give charity on her behalf." (Bukhari, Wasaya, 19; Abu Dawud, Wasaya, 15/2881)

Harithah ibn Numan -Allah be well-pleased with him-, a Companion, had lost his sight. He had a rope tied to his door and kept a basked full of dates and other things by his side. Whenever a needy person walked past and greeted him, he would grab something from the basket, and holding onto the rope, he would guide himself to the threshold of his door and personally give to the needy what he had in his hands. Time and again, his family would say to him, "There is no need for you to do that…we can give it on your behalf" but he would respond, each time:

"I heard the Messenger of Allah -upon him blessings and peace- say, 'Giving to the needy with his own hands will protect a person from an awful death!" (Ibn Saad, III, 488; Tabarani, Kabir, III, 229, 231; Haythami, III, 112)

Aisha -Allah be well-pleased with her- explains:

"The Messenger of Allah -upon him blessings and peace- once said to his wives, 'The quickest to reunite with me from among you is she with the longest arms.' We then began measuring our arms to see who had the longest. But it turned out that what was meant by 'the longest arms' was the arms that extended the most towards charity…and those belonged to Zaynab -Allah be well-pleased with her- who worked and donated with her own hands." (Muslim, Fadailu's-Sahabah, 101)

Rich or poor, ill or healthy, they all used to rally to donate.

One day, a poor person came to Othman -Allah be well-pleased with him-, complaining, "You rich people are dominating all the rewards by donating, freeing slaves and performing pilgrimage using your wealth!"

"Do you really envy us?" asked Othman -Allah be well-pleased with him-.

"Yes", replied the poor man. "By Allah, we do!"

"I promise by Allah" Othman -Allah be well-pleased with him- then began to explain, "that a dirham donated amid hardships is much better than ten-thousand dirhams donated from a greater wealth!" (Bayhaki, Shuab, III, 251; Ali al-Muttaqi, VI, 612/17098)

They Realized that there was Nothing like Fasting

"Advise me with such a deed", Abu Umamah -Allah be well-pleased with him- once asked the Blessed Prophet -upon him blessings and peace- "that Allah will reward me through it."

"I advise you with fasting, for there is nothing like it!" the Messenger of Allah -upon him blessings and peace- replied. (Nasai, Siyam, 43)

Umm Ayman -Allah be well-pleased with her- had set out to undertake her Hegira to Allah and His Messenger. She was fasting. She neither had anything to eat or drink with her, nor a mount to ride on. Slowly advancing in the scorching heat of the Tihama desert, she was on the brink of dying from thirst and hunger. Near the time of *iftar* as she was lying down exhausted, she heard a rustling sound from above her head. When she lifted her head, she saw a bucket hanging on a rope. She says, "I took the bucket and drank to my heart's content. I never felt thirsty after that."

There were times after that when Umm Ayman -Allah be well-pleased with him- would intentionally fast under boiling heat and circumambulate the Kaabah, just to see if she would feel any thirst. But she never did and that is how it remained up until her death. (Abdurrazzaq, Musannaf, IV, 309; Abu Nuaym, Hilya, II, 67; Ibn Hajar, Isabah, VIII, 170; Ibn Saad, VIII, 224)

Before setting out to the Battle of Uhud, Hamza -Allah be well-pleased with him- made an intention to fast. 'If I end up being martyred', he thought, 'I will meet my Lord while still fasting'.

Anas ibn Malik -Allah be well-pleased with him- explains:

"Whilst the Messenger of Allah -upon him blessings and peace- was alive, my stepfather Abu Talha -Allah be well-pleased with him- never used to fast a lot, apart from the compulsory fasting of Ramadan, so he could fight with greater ease during battles. But after the Prophet's -upon him blessings and peace- passing away, I never saw him not fasting, apart from the days of *eid*." (Bukhari, Jihad, 29)

Abu Talha -Allah be well-pleased with him- was among the most courageous warriors of the battlefield. He would not offer many supererogatory fasts, so that he could meet the enemy with strength. But later in life, when the battles he undertook became few and far between, he took to fasting and spent a majority of his days offering the deed. It is reported that he lived a further twenty-four years in this state following the passing away of the Blessed Prophet -upon him blessings and peace-.

As narrated by Anas -Allah be well-pleased with him-, towards the final days of his life Abu Talha -Allah be well-pleased with him- recited aloud the below *ayah*:

"Go forth light and heavy, and strive hard in Allah's way with your property and your persons; this is better for you, if you know." (at-Tawba, 41) after which he said:

"Allah the Almighty commands us to take to the battlefield, young and old. Fetch my weapons!"

"We will fight in your place, father", replied his sons. But Abu Talha -Allah be well-pleased with him- could not be calmed. So they eventually prepared his weapons, as Abu Talha -Allah be well-pleased with him- set out on a naval campaign. It was during this campaign that he breathed his last. Even though they could bury him only after seven days, his corpse showed no signs of deformation or odor. (Ibn Hajar, Fath'ul-Bari, [Jihad, 29])

Abu Burdah -Allah be well-pleased with him- and Yazid ibn Abi Kabshah once went out on a journey together. Cautious to fast as many days as he could, Yazid -Allah be well-pleased with him- was fasting this time around as well. Abu Burdah said to him:

"I heard my father Abu Musa say on numerous occasions that he heard the Messenger of Allah -upon him blessings and peace- state, 'Whosoever is ill or sets out on a journey receives the rewards of the supererogatory deeds he offers when healthy or at rest.'" (Bukhari, Jihad, 134)

During the Age of Bliss, the month of Ramadan was lived with enthusiasm and excitement and Muslims used to ensure their children also breathed this air of spirituality as much as they could. Omar -Allah be well-pleased with him- in fact once reproached a drunken man he came upon during Ramadan, saying, "Woe to you…Even our children are fasting right now!" (Bukhari, Sawm, 47)

Abu'd-Darda -Allah be well-pleased with him- expresses the importance he attached to fasting, among other things, in the words below:

"Were it not for three things, I would not have wished to remain on Earth: Prostrating to my Creator, day and night, by placing my forehead on the ground and thereby prepare for my eternal life, enduring thirst by fasting during the hottest hours of day, and spend time with people who choose the best words to speak, just as a person would pick the best fruits to eat." (Munawi, Fayz'ul-adir, II, 11/1193)

They used to Spill Over with Excitement over *Hajj* and *Umrah*

The Companions used to attach an enormous importance to pilgrimage, both *hajj* and *umrah*. They would circumambulate the Kaabah with devotion, never abandoning these deeds. They used to fill their lungs with the spiritual air of those sacred places, fill their appetites with the feast descending on the ground of both Mecca and Medina. Following the trail left by all prophets since Adem –upon him peace- and by hearts aching with love, they would replenish their spirits with their memories. With an attitude of respect towards the signs of the Divine spread out over those sacred lands, they would use every opportunity during the pilgrimage to remember the Almighty.

Bara ibn Marur -Allah be well-pleased with him-, one of the twelve representatives who took part in the First Aqabah Pledge, had promised, at the time, to come and visit the Blessed Prophet -upon him blessings and peace- and the Kaabah in the upcoming year during pilgrimage season. But before he could fulfill his promise, he found himself lying on his deathbed. Thereupon, he asked his family to at least turn him

"...towards the direction of Kaabah, for I had promised the Messenger of Allah that I would come!"

He thus became the first person to turn towards the soon-to-be *qibla* both in life and death.

Upon arriving in Medina, with a few of his Companions by his side, the Noble Messenger -upon him blessings and peace- paid a visit to Bara's -Allah be well-pleased with him- grave and offered his funeral salat. After that he prayed:

"Allah...Forgive him! Have mercy on him and be pleased with him!" (Ibn Abdilbar, I, 153; Ibn Saad, III, 619-620)

Aisha -Allah be well-pleased with her- recounts:

"I once asked the Messenger of Allah if us women could also join Muslim forces in battle and do our part in *jihad*. But he said, 'The best and the most beautiful *jihad* for you is an accepted *hajj*.' Since hearing this from him, I have never neglected it." (Bukhari, Jaza'us-Sayd, 26)

Omar -Allah be well-pleased with him- once asked the Blessed Prophet -upon him blessings and peace- permission to perform *umrah*. "My dearest brother", said he, "do not forget us in your prayers!"

"These words of the Messenger of Allah" Omar -Allah be well-pleased with him- later said regarding this compliment, "are more valuable to me than the entire world. I could not have been happier if there were to give me the whole of earth." (See, Abu Dawud, Witr, 23/1498; Tirmidhi, Daawat, 109/3562; Ibn Majah, Manasiq, 5)

The Companions would never shrink back from suffering hardships in the way of *hajj* and *umrah*. Aisha -Allah be well-pleased with her-, held back from *umrah* by menstruation, lamented to the Blessed Prophet -upon him blessings and peace-, saying:

"Others, Messenger of Allah, are returning having performed both *hajj* and *umrah* while I only *hajj*."

"Hold on", replied the Noble Messenger -upon him blessings and peace-. "Once your cycle is over, go to Tanim (with your brother Abdurrahman), enter *ihram* with an intention for *umrah* and then begin to call out the *talbiyah*. After you complete your *umrah*, come and meet us at such and such place. But know that the rewards of your *umrah* will be in proportion to wealth you spend and the hardships you endure in the process." (Bukhari, *Umrah*, 8)

The Companions were extremely polite and well-mannered during pilgrimage. Advising to behave courteously while circumambulating, the Blessed Prophet -upon him blessings and peace- had once given the below advice to Omar -Allah be well-pleased with him-:

"You are a man of strength, Omar. Do not inflict harm on the weak by pushing and shoving people to reach the Black Stone! Neither be discomfited, nor cause discomfort! If you see that it is vacant around, then touch *Hajar'ul-Aswad* and kiss it. Otherwise make a gesture from a distance and pass through saying *La ilaha ill-Allah* and *Allah'u Akbar*!" (Ahmed, I, 28; Haythami, III, 241)

Women would not mix with men while circumambulating. Aisha -Allah be well-pleased with her-, for instance, used to circumambulate a considerable distance away from men. A woman circumambulating with her once suggested they should draw closer to touch the Black Stone. But Aisha -Allah be well-pleased with her- refused.

Aisha -Allah be well-pleased with her- and her friends would even cover themselves to a point beyond recognition and circumambulate the Kaabah at night. Males would be taken out of the Sacred House when they wished to enter to worship. (Bukhari, Hajj, 64)

On one occasion, as the Blessed Prophet -upon him blessings and peace- was about to depart from Mecca, he realized that his wife Umm Salamah, undergoing her monthly cycle, had not yet circumambulated.

"When you hear the *qamah* for the *fajr* and people begin to offer the salat" he said to her, as a means through which she could fulfill her deed, "circumambulate on camelback from the outer." (Bukhari, Hajj, 71)

Umm Salamah -Allah be well-pleased with her-recounts herself:

"I informed the Messenger of Allah -upon him blessings and peace- of my situation during *hajj*. He told me to circumambulate on camelback from behind the Muslims as they offered their *salat*. Meanwhile, the Messenger of Allah -upon him blessings and peace- was leading them in fajr salat, reciting the *surah* that begins with وَالطُّورِ. وَكِتَابٍ مَسْطُورٍ (*surah* at-Tur)." (Bukhari, Hajj, 64)

We can conclude from these narrations that females may circumambulate with males, though it is better for them to do so from the outer, as much the situation permits. Circumambulating the Kaabah is a deed of worship, just like salat. Just as females stand behind males during *salat*, it is more proper for them to circumambulate in the outer rows.

They Esteemed Learning the Quran and Hadith

Allah, glory unto Him, declares:

"(It is) a Book We have revealed to you abounding in good that they may ponder over its verses, and that those endowed with understanding may be mindful." (Saad, 29)

"Surely they who recite the Book of Allah and keep up prayer and spend out of what We have given them secretly and openly, hope for a gain which will not perish." (Fatir, 29)

The Blessed Prophet -upon him blessings and peace- used to immediately recite to his Companions, first males then females, the *ayat* of the Quran that were revealed to his pure heart.[24] Some Muslims would then memorize the given revelation, while others would write it down and hang onto it.

Transcribing the Quran was a widespread practice among the Companions. Almost everyone had taken on the task. Most of those who did not know how to write would arrive at the Masjid with a marker and something to write on and get voluntary scribes to write for them what was revealed.[25]

This way, the Holy Quran was recorded and put into practice since the very first days of Islam, even when Muslims were almost crushed under the ruthless oppression of the idolaters. Omar -Allah be well-pleased with him- had in fact become Muslim by reading some parts of the Quran recorded in written form.[26]

---

24 See, Ibn Ishaq, *Sirah,* s. 128.

25 See, Bayhaki, *es-Sunanu'l-Kubra,* VI, 6.

26 See, Ibn Hisham, I, 369-371.

The Noble Messenger -upon him blessings and peace- presented a written copy of the Holy Quran, which included every single *ayah* revealed to date, to Rafi ibn Malik -Allah be well-pleased with him- during the Aqabah Pledge. After returning to Medina, Rafi -Allah be well-pleased with him- would recite them to the new Muslims, who would gather in what is known as the first mosque of Islam, which Rafi himself had built in his own neighborhood.[27]

Abdullah ibn Masud -Allah be well-pleased with him- says:

"When a Companion returned home, his wife would straight away ask him two questions: 'How many ayat were revealed today?' and 'How many of the Prophet's *ahadith* did you memorize?'" (Abdulhamid Kashk, Fi Rihabi't-Tafsir, I, 26)

The below words, again from Abdullah ibn Masud -Allah be well-pleased with him-, further bear out the strong connection the Companions had with the Quran:

"I promise by Allah, apart from Whom there is no god, that there is not a *surah* revealed from the Book of Allah, whose place of revelation is unknown

27 See, Ibn Hajar, *İsabah,* II, 189, 190; Ibn Kathir, *al-Bidayah,* III, 152; Ibn'ul-Asir, *Usdu'l-Ghabah,* II, 157; Kattani, *Taratib,* Beirut, I, 44; Prof. Dr. M. M. al-A'zami, *Kur'an Tarihi,* s. 106; Prof. Dr. M. Hamidullah, *Kur'ân-ı Kerîm Tarihi,* s. 44.

to me. Again, there is not an *ayah* revealed from the Book of Allah, without me knowing which person it was revealed about. If I heard that someone knew the Book of Allah better than I and it was possible to go to him on camelback, I would not waste anytime in setting out on the road." (Bukhari, Fadail'ul-Quran, 8)

Time and again, Abdullah ibn Masud -Allah be well-pleased with him- would recite and teach his students a certain ayah of the Quran and follow it up by saying, "This *ayah* is better than anything the Sun has ever shone upon on Earth!" He would say the same for every single *ayah*. (Haythami, VII, 166)

His below words again show just how much the Companions were occupied in training themselves in Quranic sciences:

"Whosoever desires knowledge, let him thoroughly contemplate the meanings of the Quran and concentrate on its interpretation and recital; for it contains the knowledge of past and present." (Haythami, VII, 165; Bayhaki, Shuab, II, 331)

The Companions would frequently get together to discuss the Quran and hadith.[28] The students of the *Suffa*, especially, were always at the *Masjid*, read-

28 Khatib al-Baghdadi, *al-Faqih wa'l-Mutafaqqih*, II, 126.

ing the Quran at day and discussing it amongst each other at night.[29]

Omar -Allah be well-pleased with him-, for one, focused on contemplating in order to better understand the Quran, reciting it reflectively, in a way that resulted in practice. Proof of this are his words, "I managed to complete (fully implement in my life) *surah* al-Baqara in twelve years and as thanks, I sacrificed a camel." (Qurtubi, I, 40)

Imam Malik reports that Abdullah ibn Omar -Allah be well-pleased with him- studied the *ayat* of *surah* al-Baqara alone for a complete eight years, in order properly understand and practice them. He would always read the Book with an eye to learn and practice its commands and steer clear from its prohibitions.[30]

Abu Bakr -Allah be well-pleased with him- has in fact said, "Explaining a single *ayah* of the Quran is more appealing to me than memorizing it alone." (Ibn'ul-Anbari, Kitab-u Izah'il-Waqf, I, 23)

A man once went to Zayd ibn Thabit -Allah be well-pleased with him- and asked him his opinion regarding a complete read of the Quran in a single week. "It would be good", replied the Companion, adding:

29 Bukhari, Jihad, 9; Muslim, Imarah, 147.
30 See, *Muwattaa*, Quran, 11; Kattani, *Taratib,* II, 191.

"But I take greater enjoyment from completing the Quran in fifteen days, or even twenty.[31] If you ask why, it is because that way I can thoroughly reflect on the Quran and better understand its meanings." (Muwatta', Quran, 4)

After the isolated manuscripts of the Quran were collected between two covers, Othman -Allah be well-pleased with him- encouraged people to transcribe copies of it for their personal use.[32] The underlying reason for this was the possibility that before that, Muslims might have only recorded certain *surah* or *ayat* rather than the whole. But now that the Quran was collected between two covers under the supervision of a steadfast commission, approved by thousands of *huffaz*, Muslims could at long last transcribe the Quran entire for themselves.

Ubaydullah ibn Abdullah -Allah be well-pleased with him- reports that the Medina Copy, one of the four copies of the Quran reproduced during the time of Othman -Allah be well-pleased with him-, was kept in the Masjid of Medina, read aloud each morning to the gathered Muslims.[33]

The Blessed Prophet -upon him blessings and peace- and his Righteous Caliphs sent many knowledgeable Companions to various centers of the Mus-

31 See, Ibn Abdilbarr, *Istidhkar,* II, 477.

32 See, Ibn Shabbah, *Tarîhu'l-Medîna,* s. 1002.

33 Ibn Shabbah, *Târîhu'l-Medîna,* p. 7; Ibn Kutaybah, *Ta'vîlu Muşhkili'l-Qurân,* p. 51.

lim world to teach the Quran and Sunnah.[34] Musab ibn Umayr -Allah be well-pleased with him-, for one, sent to Medina before the Hegira as a teacher, relentlessly explained Islam to her locals and read them the Quran at every given opportunity.[35]

Abu'd-Darda -Allah be well-pleased with him-, who was sent to Damascus, enjoyed a long life there, during which he founded a famous circle of knowledge. The number of his students was well above 1600. Dividing them into groups, he would assign for each group a teacher from among his better learned students and personally inspect their developments. Students who were able to pass the basic level were then given the honor of attending the circle of the illustrious Companion. That way, advanced students had the privilege of both continuing attending Abu'd-Darda's -Allah be well-pleased with him- circle and act as teacher for beginners.[36] The same method was applied elsewhere by other Companions.[37]

Omar -Allah be well-pleased with him- assigned Yazid ibn Abdullah -Allah be well-pleased with him- with the task of teaching the Quran to Bedouins dwelling in distant provinces and later Abu Sufyan -Allah be

---

34 Dârimî, *Sunan,* I, 135 (thk. Dahman); Ibn Saad, VI, 3.

35 Ibn Hisham, II, 43-46; Abû Nuaym, *Dalailu'n-Nubüwwah,* I, 307; Haythamî, VI, 41; Dhahabi, *Siyar,* I, 182.

36 Dhahabi, *Siyaru A'lâmi'n-Nubalâ,* II, 344-346.

37 Balazurî, *Ansâb,* I, 110; Hâkim, I, 220.

well-pleased with him- to inspect their levels of education. He additionally appointed three Companions to teach the Quran to the children of Medina, giving them each a salary of 15 dirhams per month, also telling them to help every person, young and old, memorize at least five from among the easier *ayat* of the Quran.[38]

Ibn Abbas -Allah be well-pleased with him- used to teach the Quran at an advanced level. People would gather around him almost everywhere he went. When he went to Basra, for instance, the first thing he reportedly did was to give a sermon to the locals, explaining them the content of *surah* al-Baqara.[39]

Ali -Allah be well-pleased with him- once heard some noises coming from the way of the Kufa Mosque and inquired as to what it was all about.

"Some people are reading and learning the Quran", he was told.

"How lovely for them", remarked he, "for they were the most beloved of all people in the sight of the Messenger of Allah." (Haythami, VII, 162)

38 Prof. Dr. M. M. al-A'zamî, *Kur'ân Tarihi,* p. 127. More detail can be found in following works: Prof. Dr. M. M. al-A'zamî, *The History of the Qur'anic Text from Revelation to Compilation: A Comparative Study with the Old and New Testaments,* Leicester: UK Islamic Academy, 2003 (*Kur'an Tarihi: Eski ve Yeni Ahit ile Karşılaştırmalı bir Araştırma,* Istanbul 2006); Prof. Dr. M. Hamidullah, *Kur'ân-ı Kerîm Tarihi,* Istanbul 2000 (The introduction to *Le Saint Coran*).

39 Hâkim, II, 300/3083.

Mujahid (d. 103 AH), one of the leading exegetes of the *Tabiun* generation, has reported that Ibn Abi Layla (d. 83 AH), a prominent jurist and scholar of hadith, *qiraah* (recital of the Quran), had set up a library consisting only of copies of the Quran, where people would gather solely for the purpose of reading the Divine Word.[40]

Abu Abdurrahman as-Sulami became a teacher of *qiraah* during the caliphate of Othman -Allah be well-pleased with him-, a profession he continued for many years. In reference to the mosque in Kufa where he was an imam and a teacher of the Quran, he would at times comment, "The only thing that keeps me here is the hope that I, too, will be considered among those praised in the hadith, 'The best of you are those who learn the Quran and teach it.'" (Bukhari, Fadail'ul-Quran, 21; Tirmidhi, Fadail'ul-Quran, 15/2907)

The *Asr-u Saadah* society showed the same vigor in learning hadith. Below is just one example.

Urwah ibn Zubayr -Allah be well-pleased with him- recounts:

"One day my aunt Aisha -Allah be well-pleased with her- said to me, 'I heard that Abdullah ibn Amr -Allah be well-pleased with him- is going to stop by us on his way to *hajj*. Meet with him and ask him

40 Ibn Saad, IV, 253; Ibn Abî Dawud, *Masâhif*, p. 151.

some questions on your mind, for he has transmitted a great deal of the knowledge of the Messenger of Allah -upon him blessings and peace-.' I thereupon met with Abdullah -Allah be well-pleased with him- and asked him many questions with regard to what he had learnt from the Prophet -upon him blessings and peace-." (Muslim, Ilm, 14)

Abdullah ibn Amr -Allah be well-pleased with him- used to record the words of the Blessed Prophet -upon him blessings and peace-, even while he was still alive. It was not long before he had compiled a great treasure of hadith.[41]

The older Companions were just as eager to expand their knowledge, in spite of having passed their prime.[42]

They would Seek their Cure from the Holy Quran

So central was the Quran in the lives of the Companions that they would resort to the words of Allah, glory unto Him, in all circumstances. When they needed to find remedies for their illnesses, it was again the Quran they would turn to.

41 Bukhari, Ilm, 39.
42 Bukhari, Ilm, 15.

Abu Said -Allah be well-pleased with him- explains:

"We were part of a military mission sent by the Messenger of Allah -upon him blessings and peace-. We stopped by at this certain place. Soon someone, with the appearance of a servant, from the nearby settlements came to us and said, 'Our chieftain has been bitten by a snake and none of us can treat him. Is there anyone from among who does *ruqyah* (reading the Quran and praying to treat an illness)?'

Then, someone from among us, whose expertise in *ruqyah* was unbeknown to us, got up and left with the person. A while later he returned with thirty sheep, given to him as thanks for healing the chieftain. We all ended up drinking their milk.

'So you do know how to do *ruqyah*?' we asked him.

'Not really', he replied. 'I simply read to him *surah* al-Fatiha.'

We then advised him not to do anything with the sheep until we had cleared the issue with the Messenger of Allah -upon him blessings and peace-. Upon returning to Medina, we immediately told him about our encounter.

'Who taught you that Fatiha is a means for *ruqyah*?' commented the Messenger of Allah -upon him blessings and peace-, adding, 'Distribute the sheep amongst yourselves and spare a share for me, too.'" (Muslim, Salam, 66, 65; Bukhari, Fadail'ul-Quran, 9; Ijarah, 16; Tibb, 33, 39)

It was only to commend the Companions' action and remove any doubts they may have had concerning payment received from medical treatment that the Blessed Prophet -upon him blessings and peace- asked them to 'spare him a share, too'. (Ayni, Umdat'ul-Qari, XXI, 271-272)

The Blessed Prophet -upon him blessings and peace- has said, in another hadith, "There is a cure for every disease in *surah* al-Fatiha." (Darimi, Fadail'ul-Quran, 12)

Ilaqa ibn Sahar -Allah be well-pleased with him- had become Muslim after meeting the Noble Messenger -upon him blessings and peace-. On the way back to his hometown, he came upon a tribe, among which there was a mentally ill man tied fast to iron bars. The man's family came to the Companion and said, "From what we hear, your friend (the Messenger of Allah -upon him blessings and peace-) has brought certain blessings. Do you know of anything that would cure this ill man?"

Ilaqa -Allah be well-pleased with him- recounts what unfolded thereafter himself:

"I then read to the man *surah* al-Fatiha. Soon, he was cured. In return, they gave me a hundred sheep. I then returned to the Messenger of Allah -upon him blessings and peace- to inform him of what had happened, to find out whether it was permissible for me to take the sheep.

'Did you read anything other than the Quran?' asked the Prophet -upon him blessings and peace-.

'No', I replied.

'Then take them', he said. 'I promise by my life that he who receives payment in return for reading from something superstitious and breathing onto a person thereof will bear its sin. But you are receiving payment in return for what is the Truth.'" (Abu Dawud, Tibb, 19/3986; Buyu', 37/3420; Ahmed, V, 211)

They used to Repent at Dawn

Allah, glory unto Him, states:

"They used to sleep but little in the night. And in the morning they asked forgiveness." (ad-Dhariyat, 17-18)

The *Asr-u Saadah* society would prefer waking up for salat at night and reciting the Quran and the names of Allah, glory unto Him, at dawn, over their warm beds. Dawn and early morning were known as "times of repentance and prayer" and were accordingly treated with sensitivity.[43] People passing by their houses at night would often hear sounds of *dhikr* and Quran recital, much like the humming of bees.

Qadi Baydawi –May Allah have mercy on him- explains this as follows:

"Once the five daily salats became compulsory for the *ummah* and the night salat voluntary (*sunnah*), the Blessed Prophet -upon him blessings and peace- stepped out of his room, at night, and walked amid the houses of his Companions, to find out what they were occupied with. He found those houses humming, like bee hives, with the sounds of the Quran and *dhikr*." (Anwar'ut-Tanzil, IV, 111)

The Blessed Prophet -upon him blessings and peace- says:

"I know very well the sounds of Quran recited by the kindhearted Ashari clan as they enter their homes at night. Even if I do not see where they stop over in their journeys during the day, I instantly recognize it from the sounds of the Quran raised by their voices at night." (Bukhari, Maghazi, 38)

Aisha -Allah be well-pleased with her- explains:

---

43 Haythami, VII, 47; Mubarakpuri, *Tuhfatu'l-Ahwazi*, II, 473-474; Ibn Hajar, *Talhisu'l-Khabir*, IV, 206.

"While in my room, the Messenger of Allah -upon him blessings and peace- awoke for the night salat (*tahajjud*) and heard the voice of Abbad ibn Abdullah, offering salat in the *Masjid* at the time.

'Is that Abbad's voice, Aisha?' he asked.

'Yes', I replied.

'Allah…Have mercy on Abbad!' he then prayed. (Bukhari, Shahadat, 11)

On eight or nine occasions, the Blessed Prophet -upon him blessings and peace- had postponed the *isha* salat to the last third of the night. Abu Bakr -Allah be well-pleased with him- then asked the Prophet -upon him blessings and peace- whether he could lead the salat a little bit earlier, so as to make it easier for them to wake up night for *tahajjud*.

The Blessed Prophet -upon him blessings and peace- complied with Abu Bakr's -Allah be well-pleased with him- wish. (Ahmed, V, 47)

Upon waking up for *tahajjud*, Omar -Allah be well-pleased with him- would pray, "My Lord…You see where I am; you know what I need. My Allah…Send me away from your presence as a servant whose needs are fulfilled, freed from all kinds of fear and threat, who immediately complies with your commands…a servant whose prayers You accepts, whose sins You forgive and on whom You treat with mercy!"

And upon completing his salat, he would pray:

"My Allah…I do not see anything on Earth that survives. Neither does it present me with an upright path I can follow. Allah…Make me a person who speaks with knowledge and who keeps silent out of wisdom! My Allah…Do not give worldly possessions in excess lest I transgress and do not completely deprive me, lest I forget my duties towards you. Surely, better are possessions that are less yet sufficient than those that are in excess and leaves one unmindful of his duties." (Ibn Abi Shaybah, Musannaf, VII, 82)

"Who does the Messenger of Allah like the most out of all people?" Aisha -Allah be well-pleased with her- was once asked.

"Fatimah", she responded.

"What about from men?" they then asked.

"Her husband", she said, "who as far as I know is a person who fasts and offers salat at night, a lot." (Tirmidhi, Manaqib, 60/3874)

Amir ibn Rabia, who had attached great importance on *tahajjud* salat throughout his life, happened to pass away while offering *tahajjud*. At the time, Muslims were on the verge of undergoing a great tribulation, only a few would survive. It was then that Amir saw someone in his dream, telling him to:

"Get up and ask Allah to protect you from the tribulation He protects His righteous servants."

He straight away awoke and offered salat. After the salat, he was instantly struck down by an illness, from which he breathed his last shortly afterwards. People came to carry his funeral out of his home, without him stepping a foot outside to join the tribulation. (Haythami, IX, 301; Ibn Abi Shaybah, Musannaf, VI, 362/32044)

With his death near, Amr ibn Abdiqays, from the *Tabiun*, began to shed tears.

"Why are you crying?" he was asked.

"I am crying neither from the fear of death nor the love of Earth", he replied. "I am crying because from now on, I will be deprived of fasting during hot days and waking up at night for the *tahajjud* salat." (Dhahabi, Siyar, IV, 19)

Below is what the people of spirituality have reportedly said about the precious time of dawn, in which deeds of worship have added value, prayers and repentances are accepted, sins are wiped off and which gives the body health:

"Reviving nights is the true kingdom and sovereignty the Almighty refers to in the *ayah*, 'Say: O Allah, Master of the Kingdom! You give the kingdom to whomsoever You please and take away the kingdom from whomsoever You please; and You exalt whom You please and abase whom You please. In Your Hand is the good; surely, You have power over all things' (Al-i Imran, 26)" (Hadimi, Majmuat'ur-Rasail (Risalatu'l-Wasiyyah wa'n-Nasihah), p. 194)

They were Diligent in their Deeds of Worship

The *Asr-u Saadah* society used to see to their obligations of worship with great diligence, though they never considered their worships to be sufficient. They always lived between fear and hope (بَيْنَ الْخَوْفِ وَالرَّجَاءِ).

Aisha -Allah be well-pleased with her- explains:

We will be able to properly return that trust which I have taken on my shoulders!" (Sarraj, Luma. p. 139)

The used to Compete in Virtue and Good Causes

The *Asr-u Saadah* society would virtually compete with each other in righteous deeds. Abdurrahman ibn Abi Bakr -Allah be well-pleased with him- explains:

"After leading the *fajr* salat, the Messenger of Allah -upon him blessings and peace- turned around facing his Companions and asked, 'Is there anyone fasting today?'

‘I did not intend on fasting yesterday evening, Messenger of Allah, so I am not fasting today’, Omar -Allah be well-pleased with him- said.

‘I intended on fasting yesterday evening and I have begun the day fasting, Messenger of Allah’, then said Abu Bakr -Allah be well-pleased with him-.

‘Has anyone paid an ill person a visit today?’ then asked the Messenger of Allah -upon him blessings and peace-.

‘We have just offered *fajr* salat, Messenger of Allah, and we have not yet moved from our spots’, said Omar -Allah be well-pleased with him-. ‘So how can we have visited an ill person?’

‘I heard brother Abdurrahman ibn Awf was ill, Messenger of Allah. So I visited him on the way to the Masjid, gave him my well-wishes and came to the Masjid from there’, confessed Abu Bakr -Allah be well-pleased with him-.

‘Has anyone among you fed a poor today?’ then inquired the Messenger of Allah -upon him blessings and peace- once more.

‘We have just offered *fajr* salat, Messenger of Allah, and we have not yet moved from our spots’, repeated Omar -Allah be well-pleased with him-.

But Abu Bakr -Allah be well-pleased with him- said, 'On the way to the *Masjid*, I came across someone who said he was in need. There was a piece of barley bread in the hands of my son Abdurrahman. I took it from his hands and gave it to him'.

'I give you the glad tidings of Paradise', the Messenger of Allah -upon him blessings and peace- then stated.

Letting out a deep sigh, Omar -Allah be well-pleased with him- remarked, 'Ah…Paradise!'

After counseling Omar -Allah be well-pleased with him- with some pleasing words, the Messenger of Allah -upon him blessings and peace- said, 'May Allah have mercy on Omar; may Allah have mercy on Omar! Whenever he wishes to do something good, Abu Bakr always leaves him in his wake!' (Haythami, III, 163-164; also see, Abu Dawud, Zakat, 36/1670; Hakim, I, 571/1501)

This teaches us the necessity of living each moment with an eye for the pleasure of Allah, glory unto Him, and that the consequences of our action will always be in line with out intentions.

The Quran declares:

"So when you are relieved, still toil. And strive to please your Lord." (al-Inshirah, 7-8)

They Would Follow the Sunnah Inch for Inch

Fudayl ibn Iyad –May Allah have mercy on Him- says:

"A deed done with sincerity (*ikhlas*) will not be accepted unless its requirements (*shurut*) are satisfied. A deed whose requirements are satisfied is still not accepted if it lacks sincerity. It will remain unaccepted, so long as the satisfaction of its requirements and sincerity remain separated from one another. Sincerity is for the deed to be fulfilled for the pleasure of Allah, glory unto Him, alone while the correct way of satisfying its requirements is for it to comply with the Sunnah."[44]

Indeed, to obey the Blessed Prophet -upon him blessings and peace- is to obey the Almighty, as indicated by the *ayah*:

"Whoever obeys the Messenger, he indeed obeys Allah, and whoever turns back, so We have not sent you as a keeper over them." (an-Nisa, 80)

Having come to grips with this truth, the *Asr-u Saadah* person would take extreme care to comply with the Sunnah of the Blessed Prophet -upon him blessings and peace- in all action and behavior.

44 Ibn Qayyim al-Jawziyyah, *A'lamu'l-Muwaqqîn*, Beirut, 1996, II, 159.

To a group of young men who had come for advice, Jabir -Allah be well-pleased with him- had in fact said:

"The Messenger of Allah -upon him blessings and peace- was among us. The Quran would be revealed to him and he would know its meaning inside out. In whichever way he practiced the Quran, we would follow him and practice it the same way." (Muslim, Hajj, 147)

Umayya ibn Abdullah had once commented to Abdullah ibn Omar -Allah be well-pleased with him- that they were "able to find in the Quran the ways of offering the salat of fear (*salat'ul-khawf*) yet the same did not apply to the salat offered in journey."

"Allah the Almighty sent us the Messenger of Allah -upon him blessings and peace- when we did not know anything. *We do exactly the same as what we saw him do*!" replied Abdullah ibn Omar –Allah be well-pleased with him-. (Ibn Majah, Iqamah, 73; Ahmed, II, 65, 94; IV, 78)

The Quran in fact states:

"O you who believe! Put not yourselves forward before Allah and His Messenger; but fear Allah: for Allah is He Who hears and knows all things." (al-Hujurat, 1)

Said ibn Musayyab, a prominent *Tabiun* scholar, saw someone offer two *rakat* of supererogatory salat after the salat of *asr*, which left the scholar displeased. Realizing his displeasure, the man tried to defend his actions by saying, "Will the Almighty ever punish me for worshipping?"

"No, the Almighty will certainly not punish you for worshipping", replied Ibn Musayyab, "but He will for your defiance of the Sunnah!" (Darimi, Muqaddimah, 38/442)

Ali -Allah be well-pleased with him- was a pillar in following the Sunnah of the Blessed Prophet -upon him blessings and peace-. He was once asked whether or not a person could ride a camel he was taking to pilgrimage for sacrifice.

"He certainly can", he replied. "Coming across people in similar situations, the Messenger of Allah -upon him blessings and peace- had commanded them to ride their camels, sacrificial or not. You could never find a way more beautiful and virtuous than the Sunnah of our Beloved Prophet -upon him blessings and peace- or pursue something better." (Ahmed, I, 121)

The below meaningful words are also from Ali –Allah be well-pleased with him-:

"We saw the Messenger of Allah -upon him blessings and peace- stand and we stood…We saw him sit and we sat." (Ahmed, I, 83)

"Apart from the one that follows the Prophet's -upon him blessings and peace- trail, all roads are blocked to mankind." (Bursawi, Ruh'ul-Bayan, [an-Nisa, 28])

After taking wudu and applying stroking over his *mas'h*, Ali –Allah be well-pleased with him- is narrated to have said, "Had I not seen the Messenger of Allah -upon him blessings and peace- do it this way, I would have thought that stroking underneath them would be more proper." (Ahmed, I, 148, 95m 124)

Abdullah ibn Awfa -Allah be well-pleased with him- made *takbir* four times during his daughter's funeral salat. Following the fourth, he stood and prayed for her forgiveness. The congregation behind him assumed he would make a fifth *takbir* but instead he gave a *salam* towards his right and left and concluded the salat.

"What is this that you did?" he was afterwards asked.

"I have not added anything to what I saw the Messenger of Allah -upon him blessings and peace- do", he replied. "This was the exact way he did it." (See, Hakim, I, 360; Ibn Majah, Janaiz, 24)

Once, struck down with a sudden illness, Abu Musa al-Ashari -Allah be well-pleased with him- had fallen unconscious, with his head resting on his wife's lap. She then let out a loud scream and began crying.

But Abu Musa al-Ashari -Allah be well-pleased with him- was too fatigued to prevent her. But the moment he regained full consciousness, he warned her, saying, "I detest and stand distant from anything the Messenger of Allah -upon him blessings and peace- detested and stood distant from. He was distant from wailing women who pull and shred their own hair and clothes from grief." (Bukhari, Janaiz, 37, 38; Muslim, Iman, 167; Nasai, Janaiz, 17)

What a sensitivity of faith it is that one should still be striving to comply with the commands of the Blessed Prophet -upon him blessings and peace- even when possibly on the brink of death.

Upon returning from any given campaign or journey, the Noble Messenger -upon him blessings and peace- would always go first to the *Masjid.* Only after offering two *rakat* of salat there would he go home. Ibn Omar -Allah be well-pleased with him- did exactly the same throughout his life.[45]

After completing *hajj* or *umrah*, Ibn Omar -Allah be well-pleased with him- would halt his camel and rest awhile in Batha near Zulhulayfah, only because the Blessed Prophet -upon him blessings and peace- did the same.[46] Likewise, Ibn Omar -Allah be well-pleased with him- would lead the salats of *zuhr*, *asr*,

45 Abu Dawud, Jihad 166/2781, 2782.

46 Bukhari, Hajj, 38, 29, 148, 149; Muslim, Hajj, 226; *Muwattaa*, Hajj, 6.

maghrib and *isha* at Muhassab[47] on time and then take a light nap. After waking up, he would inform people that the Blessed Prophet used to do the same.[48]

The Noble Prophet -upon him blessings and peace- had once purchased his sacrificial camel at Qudayd, located on the road from Medina to Mecca. So did Ibn Omar -Allah be well-pleased with him-, in like manner.[49]

To people asking him why he would do something in a certain manner, his answer would remain unchanged:

"*It is because I saw the Messenger of Allah do it this way.*"[50]

Abu Rafi recounts:

"I offered an isha salat behind the lead of Abu Hurayrah -Allah be well-pleased with him-. He read *surah* al-Inshiqaq and went down to prostrate. I asked him the reason why he did and he answered, 'I prostrated behind the lead of the Messenger of Allah to

47 Muhassab is located between Mina and Mecca, somewhat closer to Mina.

48 Bukhari, Hajj, 149; Muslim, Hajj, 337; *Muwattaa*, Hajj, 207.

49 Tirmidhi, Hajj, 68/907.

50 Bukhari, Vudû' 30, Hajj 16, 38, 149; Muslim, Hajj 25, 245, 521, Alfaz 21; Tirmidhi, Hajj 39/864; Abu Dawud, Khatam 5/4227, 4228; Nasâî, Hajj 174; Ibn Mâjah, Hajj 43; *Muwattaa*, Hajj 31.

this surah…and I shall continue to do so until I die.'" (Muslim, Masajid, 110; Ahmed, II, 229)

Abu Harun al-Abdi explains:

"As young men, we used to go to Abu Said in hope of learning some things from him. Seeing us, he would remark, 'The people whom the Messenger of Allah -upon him blessings and peace- has left with us as legacy and entrusted us with…Welcome all! Indeed, the Prophet -upon him blessings and peace- did say to us:

'People will follow you. They will come from all corners of the world, seeking to learn the religion and become deeper in their knowledge of it. Attend to them when they come to you and treat these seekers of knowledge with goodness and beauty.'" (Tirmidhi, Ilm, 4/2650; Ibn Majah, Muqaddima, 17, 22; Darimi, Muqaddimah, 26; Hakim, I, 164/298)

A woman of the tribe of Ghifar had asked the Blessed Prophet -upon him blessings and peace- how she could clean bloodstains from her dress.

"Take a container of water," he advised "sprinkle some salt inside and wash the stain with it". Throughout her life, the woman devotedly followed this advice, never washing her clothes without sprinkling some salt into the water. She even willed for her corpse to be washed with saltwater before her death. (Abu Dawud, Taharah, 122/313)

Such was the *Asr-u Saadah* generation. Complying with the Prophet's -upon him blessings and peace- advices and words and imitating his every deed with loyalty, diligence and sensitivity had become for them the greatest and most zestful source of joy thinkable.

Moral Maturity in the Age of Bliss

Moral Maturity in the Age of Bliss

The age of Bliss is undoubtedly the most exceptional period in the history of mankind, typified by virtue, selflessness and moral excellence. It was that period in which the Blessed Prophet -upon him blessings and peace-, the reason for the existence of entire creation, graced the earth. It was a period molded and inspired by his behavior and spirituality. That age was, again, a time of getting to know the Almighty and His Messenger, with love and ecstasy, in an environment of deep contemplation.

Let's think of a great mountain…From a distance, it appears as a silhouette, somewhat vague. But the closer one gets, the more visible the trees, the fruits, chirping birds and streams flowing through it become. Admiration for it only grows with each step taken towards it.

Similarly, getting to know the Noble Messenger -upon him blessings and peace- in the truest sense is impossible merely by reading about him from books. He can only be known through the love one carries in his heart and only through that love may one get closer to him. It was with such love that the Companions conducted themselves towards the Blessed Prophet -upon him blessings and peace-, responding to his every wish with the sincere words:

"May my mother, father, everything I have and even my very own life be ransomed in your way, Messenger of Allah!"

The best indication of our love for the Blessed Prophet -upon him blessings and peace- is our love for the Quran and the Sunnah, the two things left in our trust as expressed in the hadith.[51] We must therefore seek to implement the Quran and Sunnah in all aspects of our lives and strive to earn the pleasure of Allah, glory unto Him, and the love of His Messenger, on the illumined path they invite us to take. By living the Quran and Sunnah, we must seek to embody the beautiful morals of Islam and make every effort to infuse society with it.

They were Peaks of Humbleness

The higher the Companions rose through Islamic morals, the more amazingly humble they became. Below is typical example:

51 See, Ibn Hisham, IV, 276; *Muwattaa*, Qadar, 3.

Salman Farisi -Allah be well-pleased with him- was the governor of Madain when a man, from the Taym Clan, arrived from Damascus with a sack of figs. He saw Salman -Allah be well-pleased with him-, whom he was unable to recognize, in great part due to the modest woolen cloak he was wearing at the time.

"Come, help me carry this load", he called out to Salman -Allah be well-pleased with him-, thinking he was a slave.

Salman -Allah be well-pleased with him- went next to him, putting the sack over his shoulders without protest. It was not long before the Damascene was told who he really was.

"That man is the governor of Madain", they said.

"Please, forgive me", then said the man apologetically. "I could not recognize you".

"No harm done", replied Salman -Allah be well-pleased with him-, modestly as ever. "I will carry the load to wherever it is that you want me to take it." (Ibn Saad, IV, 88)

The Almighty praises His modest servants, like Salman Farisi -Allah be well-pleased with him-, in the Quran as follows:

"The (faithful) servants of the Beneficent are they who walk upon the earth modestly, and when the foolish ones address them answer: Peace..." (al-Furqan, 63)

They were Oceans of Compassion

Compassion was one of the most distinctive attributes of the *Asr-u Saadah* society. The incident below shows the supreme level of compassion and benevolence attained to by the Companions, young and old:

Walking through the vineyards of Medina, Hasan -Allah be well-pleased with him- once saw a black slave holding a bread in his hand, eating some of it himself, while feeding some to a dog in front of him.

"Who are you, young man?" Hasan -Allah be well-pleased with him- asked.

"I am a servant of Aban ibn Othman" replied the young man.

"Then to whom does this vineyard belong?"

"To Aban…"

"Do not leave", Hasan -Allah be well-pleased with him- then said. "I will return in a moment!"

Hasan -Allah be well-pleased with him- then hurriedly went next to Aban, the owner of the vineyard, and purchased both the vineyard and the slave from him. He then arrived by the side of the slave once more:

"I have purchased you, young man", he said.

"Very well," said the young man in a respectful tone. "Then it is my duty to obey Allah and His Messenger, and you..."

Hasan -Allah be well-pleased with him- got all the more emotional upon hearing these words and he said:

"For Allah's sake, from now on you are free...and the vineyard is yours as present!"

"In that case", replied the young man, "I leave this vineyard to the Almighty, for the sake of Whom you have just set me free!" (Ibn Manzur, Muhtasaru Tarihi Dimashq, VII, 25)

The young man, seemingly a slave yet clearly a pillar of spirituality, thereby responded to virtue with virtue, in return for the mercy and generosity he was treated with.

Abdullah ibn Mubarak (d. 181 AH), a leading hadith scholar of the Tabiun generation, was a well-to-do man. Accompanied by his friends, he once set out for pilgrimage. On the way, he noticed two little girls, living in a small hut by the road. Left on their own without anyone to take care of them, the two girls reached their hands towards a dead bird lying nearby, to satisfy their hunger. Seeing this unfold right before his eyes, Abdullah ibn Mubarak decided not to continue his journey. He spared some twenty dinars of the thousand he had with him for his return trip to Damascus, while handing the rest to the two girls.

"Why are you doing this?" his friends asked him, to which he replied, "This will reap more rewards than our pilgrimage for this year."[52]

While offering salat one day, Hadrat Rabi ibn Haytham had his horse, worth twenty-thousand dinars, stolen right before his eyes. But instead of pursuing the thief, he chose to continue his peaceful salat. Hearing his great loss, his friends came running to console him.

"You know, I did notice the thief as he was untying the horse's reins," he said to them. "But I was preoccupied with something much more important at the time, a deed I truly love. So that is why I did not run after the thief."

They then began to curse the thief, only to be silenced by Rabi himself.

"Calm down…Nobody has wronged me. The thief has simply wronged himself. Let's not add salt to his wound, as if what the poor man inflicted upon himself was not enough." (Bkz. Babanzâde Ahmed Naîm, *İslâm Ahlâkının Esasları,* s. 85-86)

52 M. Said Hatiboğlu, "İlk Sûfîlerin Hadis/Sünnet Anlayışı Üzerine" *İslâmiyat,* v. 2, no. 3, July-September, 1999, p. 13.

The poem says it brilliantly:

Run, with Your mercy, when a Believer is in peril,

And spare the better part of your mercy for the doer of evil

The people of the *Asr-u Saadah* were also exemplary in their compassion towards animals and plants. The Blessed Prophet -upon him blessings and peace- had once come across a man milking his sheep. He told him to:

"Leave some milk for its lambs." (Haythami, VIII, 196)

On one occasion, Abu'd-Darda -Allah be well-pleased with him- happened upon a few men loading their camels with too much weight. One camel could not even manage to stand. After unloading the excess load from the camel's back and helping it to stand, Abu'd-Darda said, to them:

"If Allah the Almighty forgives you the pain you have caused on your camels, He will surely have shown an enormous mercy…for I have heard the Messenger of Allah -upon him blessings and peace- say, 'Allah commands you to treat these mute creatures well! If you pass through fertile soil, let them graze a little! If you pass through arid soil, pass through it quickly and do not cause them distress by lingering there." (Ibn Hajar, al-Matalibu'l-Aliyah, II, 226/1978)

They Loved Forgiving for the Sake of the Almighty

One must always forgive others, so that the Almighty, too, forgives him. We have all committed errors, be it against the Creator or other human beings, waiting to be forgiven.

Abu Bakr -Allah be well-pleased with him- used to lend frequent aid to a poor man called Mistah. Seeing Mistah, too, was among the defamers during the *Ifk* Incident, a slander leveled against the honorable Aisha -Allah be well-pleased with her-, he vowed never again to help him or his family. But then the Almighty revealed:

"And let not those of you who possess grace and abundance swear against giving to the near of kin and the poor and those who have fled in Allah's way, and they should pardon and turn away. Do you not love that Allah should forgive you? And Allah is Forgiving, Merciful." (an-Nur, 22)

"Of course, I would want Allah to forgive me", said Abu Bakr -Allah be well-pleased with him- upon hearing the *ayah*. Compensating (*kaffarah*) for his oath, he then resumed the charity like before. (Bukhari, Maghazi, 34; Muslim, Tawba, 56; Tabari, Tafsir, II, 546)

As Caliph, Ali –Allah be well-pleased with him- wrote an edict for Malik ibn Harith, appointed as the governor of Egypt. The below words, taken from that edict, give us a wonderful idea of what the *Asr-u Saadah* person understood from the term 'to forgive':

"Do not look upon human beings like a wolf looks upon a flock of sheep! Nurture in your heart feelings of love, mercy and kindness towards them, for all human beings are either your brothers or sisters in religion or your equal in creation. They may make mistakes or undergo troubles. Hold the weak by the hand...and if you want Allah to forgive you then forgive and be lenient towards others! Do not ever defy Allah! Do not regret it should you forgive, and do not rejoice should you hand out a punishment!" [53]

Recounting an instance of compassion that left him speechless is Isam ibn Mustaliq:

"I had come to Medina. Soon, I caught a glimpse of Hasan -Allah be well-pleased with him-, the son of Ali –Allah be well-pleased with him-. I was deeply impressed by his lovely appearance and stately manners. But this only fuelled the fire of jealousy deep inside me, owing to a hidden grudge I was holding at the time against his father. Without mentioning his father's name, I asked him:

'Are you Abu Talib's grandson?'

As soon as he said 'Yes', I began to curse both him and his father, using words one would think

53 Muhyiddîn Seydî Çelebi, *Buhârî'de Yönetim Esasları,* prepared by Doç. Dr. Mehmet Erdoğan, Istanbul 2000, p. 47.

twice before uttering. Meanwhile, Hasan -Allah be well-pleased with him- was just staring at me with a most remarkable look of compassion. After saying the *Basmalah*, he then recited the *ayat*:

'Take to forgiveness and enjoin good and turn aside from the ignorant. And should a false suggestion from the Shaytan afflict you, seek refuge in Allah; surely He is Hearing, Knowing. When a visitation from the Shaytan afflicts those who guard against evil, they remember and suddenly they discern!' (al-Araf, 199-201)

He then gave me the following advice:

'Prefer discretion! Seek forgiveness from Allah for both if us! For if you were to ask help from us, we would not hesitate. If you were to ask us to have you as guest, we would lovingly do so. And if you were to ask us to teach you, we would do our best to show you the right way!'

When he realized from my expression that I had deeply regretted my words, he then read the *ayah*:

'...There shall be no reproof against you this day; Allah may forgive you, and He is the most Merciful of the merciful!' (Yusuf, 92)

'Are you from Damascus?' he then inquired, becoming conscious of the fact that I was a supporter of Muawiyah. When I replied 'Yes' he read me a wonderful poem, describing how he was no stranger to being treated harshly by Damascenes.

Then full of warmth and sincerity, he said, 'Welcome…Allah's peace upon you! May Allah give you health and power, and may He help you! If you ever feel in need, do not feel shy, tell us. Ask from us whatever it is that comes to your mind. *Insh-Allah* you will see that we are better than what you think of us!'

I felt embarrassed. I wished the Earth to open up and swallow me. I then moved away, out of sight. But one thing was for sure. After that point, nobody was dearer to me than Ali and Hasan -Allah be well-pleased with him-um.'" (Qurtubi, Tafsir, [al-Araf, 201])

Man is always defeated by kindness, as stated in the Quran:

"And good and evil are not equal. Repel evil with what is best, and suddenly he with whom you had enmity, would be as if he were a warm friend." (Fussilat, 34)

This amazing incident shows the wonderful effects of good morals. Winning hearts by forgiving and thereby putting Islamic morals on display, can exercise an enormous influence on others.

Mamun ibn Mihran was a Tabiun scholar, dedicated to worshipping. One evening, as he had guests over his house for dinner, his servant tripped and spilt the hot food on him. Burnt and in pain, Mamun became visibly angry. Fearing the consequences of this tricky situation, the servant said:

"All you can do now, master, is to fulfill the Almighty's command and 'choke back your anger'".[54]

"I have", replied Mamun and he instantly calmed down. Heartened, the servant continued referring to the same *ayah*.

"You should also observe the command to 'forgive others'".

"Sure", replied Mamun. "I forgive you!"

The servant then continued with the rest of the ayah, reminding him how Allah, glory unto Him, loves the generous (*muhsin*).

"Then so shall I treat you generously", remarked Mamun. "For the sake of Allah, from now on, you are free!" (Kurtubi, IV, 207, [Al-i Imran, 134])[55]

They Had Their Share of Two Prophetic Attributes: Trustworthiness *(al-Amin)* and Loyalty *(as-Sadiq)*

When the Blessed Prophet -upon him blessings and peace- gave a large amount of the spoils of Hunayn to Meccans in hope of warming them to Islam, feeling unsettled, some young Ansari Companions remarked,

54 Al-i Imran, 134.

55 According to another report, the person in question was not M -mun ibn Mihran but Jafar as-Sadiq.

"This is amazing! Our swords still drip of Qurayshi blood and in return, they are receiving our spoils!"

When the Noble Messenger -upon him blessings and peace- became aware of the resentment, he gathered the Ansari men and asked:

"Is it true that you have been saying these things?"

By now, the said Companions were deeply embarrassed and remorseful over their words. Still, with their heads bowed, they replied, "Yes…We have said exactly what you have heard!"

It was simply because they never spoke a lie. (Muslim, Zakat, 134)

Even the sworn enemies of Islam would admire Muslim trustworthiness and take their word. In the aftermath of the Battle of Uhud, Abu Sufyan, the commander of the army of idolaters, called to Omar –Allah be well-pleased with him- from a distance, asking curiously:

"Answer me, Omar, in the name of Allah…Did we really kill Muhammad?"

"I promise by Allah that you did not", responded Omar –Allah be well-pleased with him. "He is listening to you as we speak!" Abu Sufyan thereupon declared:

"I have more trust in your words, Omar, than our own Ibn Kamia who informed us of having killed him!" (Ibn Hisham, III, 45; Waqidi, I, 296-297; Ahmed, I, 288; Haythami, VI, 111)

This is an incredible display. An idolater confesses trust in the words of not another fellow idolater who just fought a battle with him, shoulder to shoulder, but of a Muslim with whom he just locked swords with. Though as incredible as this is, it is only natural, since human beings are infatuated by a quality of character; and they place full trusts in persons they see as possessing that quality.

A delegate from Yemen had arrived to the Blessed Prophet –upon him blessings and peace-, requesting him to send them a Companion to teach them "Islam and the Sunnah". Holding Abu Ubaydah ibn Jarrah –Allah be well-pleased with him- the Blessed Prophet –upon him blessings and peace- thereupon said:

"This man is the most trustworthy of my people", and sent the Companion away with the Yemenis. (Muslim, Fadailu's-Sahabah, 54; Ahmad, III, 146)

The above incident further highlight the enormous virtue that lies in being loyal and trustworthy; so much so that it elicits the personal praises of the Prophet –upon him blessings and peace-.

They were Winds of Mercy in Generosity and Selflessness

Reared by the Blessed Prophet –upon him blessings and peace-, the Companions had also acquired a great share of his generosity and selflessness.

"I do not know a single person from either the Ansar or the Muhajirun", said Jabir –Allah be well-pleased with him- "who did not donate a trust." (Ibn Qudamah, al-Mughni, V, 598)

Ibn Hazm says:

"Many Companions including Abdullah ibn Omar and Fatimah –Allah be well-pleased with them- had donated numerous trusts in and around Medina. This is common knowledge; there is not a single person who does not know of this." (M. Abduh Yemani, Fatimatu'z-Zahra, Beirut, 1996, p. 330)

The illustrious Muslim commander Khalid ibn Walid –Allah be well-pleased with him- had even donated his swords, shields and all military equipment as trust in the way of Allah, glory unto Him. (Bukhari, Zakat, 49, 33; Jihad, 89; Muslim, Zakat, 11)

Ubaydullah ibn Abbas –Allah be well-pleased with him- had set out on a journey, accompanied by his servant, a former slave who he had set free. On the way, they noticed a Bedouin's house.

"How about we go to that house over there?" Ubaydullah suggested to his servant. "We might rest there…and perhaps even spend the night."

So they went. Ubaydullah was a stately man of poise; and the moment the Bedouin saw him in front of his door, he felt a natural liking towards him.

"We have an honorable guest!" he called out to his wife.

After welcoming his guests and making them comfortable, the Bedouin returned to his wife and asked her whether they had anything to offer their guests.

"Nothing except for that sheep over there…which our little daughter depends on for her daily milk", she said despondently.

"We have to slaughter it!" said the Bedouin.

"That would be like killing our daughter!" she answered.

"So be it then", replied the resolute Bedouin.

Laying the sheep on the ground, the Bedouin then grabbed a knife, and improvised a short poem:

Do not wake my girl…asleep

For she will take my knife and weep

He then slit the sheep's throat and prepared a stew from its meat, which he placed in front of Ubaydullah and his servant. The sensitive Ubaydullah had overheard the conversation between the Bedouin and his wife. Next morning, Ubaydullah asked his servant whether they had any money with them.

"Yes…around fife hundred dinars left over from our travel expenses", he informed.

"Give all of it to the Bedouin", Ubaydullah said.

"The entire five hundred?" asked the puzzled servant. "He only slaughtered five dinar worth sheep for you!"

"Shame on you!" replied Ubaydullah. "Make no mistake that he is much more generous than we are. We are only giving him a portion of what we have. Yet, he gave us all of what he had…he preferred our comfort to her daughter's life. Nothing we can do can ever compensate that!"

When Muawiyah heard about the incident, he remarked, "What a great man Ubaydullah is…he just showed just whose son he is and which house he grew up in!" (Ibnu'l-Asir, Usdu'l-Ghabah, Beirut, 1417, III, 543; Ibn Asakir, Tarikhu Dimashq, XXXVII, 483-484)

Ubaydullah was the son of Abbas –Allah be well-pleased with them-, the uncle of the Blessed Prophet –upon him blessings and peace-.

While fasting one day, a needy man came to the door of Aisha –Allah be well-pleased with her- and asked her for something to eat. She had nothing but a piece of bread.

"Give the man the bread", she said to her servant.

"But you have nothing else to break your fast with", the servant replied.

"Give it to him still", insisted Aisha -Allah be well-pleased with her-. What unfolded after that is recounted by the servant:

"I gave the bread to the poor man. At sunset, someone then sent us some cooked mutton to Aisha -Allah be well-pleased with her-. She called me and said:

'Help yourself…this sure is tastier than your loaf of bread!'" (Muwatta, Sadaqah, 5)

It is reported that Ibn Omar -Allah be well-pleased with him- would not sit down to eat unless accompanied by an orphan to join him. (Bukhari, al-Adabu'l-Mufrad, no: 136; Abu Nuaym, Hilyah, I, 299)

The great Hasan Basri, who had the good fortune of seeing many Companions, once said:

"I witnessed such times that upon waking up in the morning, a Muslim would urge his family to '…Take care of the orphans and the needy in your neighborhood!' And today, the good men have passed on and you are becoming morally weaker by the day." (Bukhari, Adabu'l-Mufrad, no: 139)

They Would Avoid Wasting

Aqil ibn Abi Talib –Allah be well-pleased with him- was one day narrating the saying of the Blessed Prophet –upon him blessings and peace- that said:

"A mudd of water is enough for ablution…and a sa' to wash your entire body".[56]

A man present then commented, "That much water is not enough for us!" Then referring to the Noble Prophet –upon him blessings and peace-, Aqil said:

"That much water was enough for a man better and with more hair than you!" (Ibn Majah, Taharah, 1)

Kathir ibn Ubayd, the freed slave of Abu Bakr and the foster brother of Aisha –Allah be well-pleased with them-, recounts:

"I once went next to Aisha, who told me to wait outside so she could finish sewing up her dress. I then remarked, 'I would tell others what you were doing, if not for the fear they might call you a miser'.

'You mind your own business', she replied. 'He who does not wear old clothes, never gets to enjoy new ones!'" (Bukhari, Adabu'l-Mufrad, no: 471; Ibn Saad, VIII, 50)

---

56 One unit of *sa'* equal four *mudds*; that is 3, 328 kgs.

لقد كان لكم في رسول الله أسوة حسنة

Social Life in the Age of Bliss

They Attached Great Importance to Islamic Education

The Blessed Prophet –upon him blessings and peace- would make the most of every opportunity to spread literacy. The ransom fee, for instance, he placed on the literate prisoners of Badr was that they each teach ten Muslim children how to read and write. The schools in which this learning was offered by teachers both Muslim and non-Muslim were called *Kuttab*.[57] Many *kuttab* were launched during that period to teach children to read and write, as well as the basics of Islam.[58]

The Companions had also turned their houses into schools. As the Suffa training offered in the Mosque of Medina could not meet the excess demands, schools referred to as *Daru'l-Qura* were opened in some

57 M. Hamidullah, *Islam Peygamberi*, I, 141.
58 A. Shalabi, *Tarîkhu't-Tarbiyati'l-Islamiyyah*, Cairo, 1960, p. 38-39.

houses in the town. Practically, Mahrama ibn Nawfal's -Allah be well-pleased with him- entire house was turned into a *Daru'l-Qura*, where Abdullah ibn Ummi Maktum -Allah be well-pleased with him- stayed as guest to undertake the teaching responsibilities.[59]

The Noble Messenger -upon him blessings and peace- had once placed a captive from the Hawazin tribe under the custody of Ali -Allah be well-pleased with him- so that he could teach the man some selected chapters of the Quran. (Ibnu'l-Asir, Usdu'l-Ghabah, VII, 105; Ibn Hajar, al-Isabah, IV, 292)

Their Trade Ethics was Exceptional

Jarir ibn Abdullah -Allah be well-pleased with him- wanted to purchase a horse from the bazaar. He saw a horse he liked, which the owner said he was prepared to let go for five-hundred dinars. But Jarir -Allah be well-pleased with him- told the man he could offer six-hundred dinars and even increase the price up to eight-hundred; as the horse was a pure-bread and worth more than the owner knew.

"Why on earth are you increasing the price" asked the astounded owner "when you can buy the horse for a lot cheaper?"

59 Kattanî, *Tarâtib,* I, 56; Ibn Abdilbarr, *al-Istîab,* I, 247; Maqridî, *al-M - waiz wa'l-Itibar bi-Dhikri'l-Hıtati wa'l-Asar,* II, 362, Egypt, 1270h.

"...For we promised the Messenger of Allah" Jabir solemnly replied "that we would never cheat in trade."[60]

Both the Blessed Prophet –upon him blessings and peace- and the righteous caliphs who followed, kept the market under close surveillance, closing all the paths to unfair revenue. To prevent the emergence of a financially dominant class, the Blessed Prophet –upon him blessings and peace- prohibited traders from monopolizing strategic spots in the market, and even had the tent of a trader, who failed to comply, torn down.[61]

Their Brotherhood was Legendary

Given the Blessed Prophet –upon him blessings and peace- was unable to see one of his brethren of religion for three days, he would ask about his wellbe ing. If on a journey, he would pray for his wellbeing. If he was at home or ill, he would make sure to pay him a visit.[62]

The Blessed Prophet –upon him blessings and peace- later established 'a pact of brotherhood' in Medina, between the local *Ansar* and the immigrant

60 Ibn Hazm, al-Muhalla, Egypt, 1389, IX, p. 454.

61 Samhudi, Wafa, Egypt, 1327, I, 540.

62 Haythami, II, 295.

Muhajirun, who had abandoned all their wealth and belongings in Mecca for the sake of their religion. This momentous sacrifice was complemented by a sacrifice of almost equal caliber. Each immigrant family was boarded in the house of a Medinan. The Companions who were declared brothers were thus to work together and share what they earned.

The *Ansar* even donated their excess land to the Blessed Prophet -upon him blessings and peace-, with the wish that he divide them amongst the *Muhajirun.* Still discontented, the *Ansar* went so far as to insist the Messenger of Allah -upon him blessings and peace- to:

"...divide our date fields amongst our immigrant brothers as well!"

"That cannot be", the Noble Prophet -upon him blessings and peace- said, upon which the *Ansar* then made the following proposal to the *Muhajirun*:

"Then you undertake the work of watering and taking care of the trees and we will split the harvest!" With the approval of the Blessed Prophet -upon him blessings and peace-, both sides agreed to the deal. (Bukhari, Harth, 5)

Recalling the below incident is Jabir -Allah be well-pleased with him-:

"Upon collecting the dates, the *Ansar* would divide them into two heaps, piling more on one side than the other. Then placing some date leaves over the smaller pile to make it look more sizable than the other, they would tell the *Muhajirun* to take whichever pile they preferred. And they, wishing for their *Ansari* brothers to take the greater pile, would choose the supposedly smaller pile, through which they would end up with most of the dates. The *Ansar* would have their wishes fulfilled by sparing for their own the smaller pile. This generous deed of the *Ansar* continued until the capture of Khaybar." (Haythami, X, 40)

The Prophet –upon him blessings and peace- once invited the *Ansar* ahead of the *Muhajirun* to distribute the lands of Bahrain. Yet, with their usual selflessness, they urged:

"Please, do not give us anything, Messenger of Allah, until you have given the *Muhajirun* double the land you have in mind for us!" The Blessed Prophet –upon him blessings and peace- thereupon said:

"Since, *Ansar*, you do not wish to take anything (for preferring your brethren over yourselves), then remain patient (with the tribulations of the world) until you reunite with me by the Pool of *Kawthar*. For there will soon come a time, after me, when others will be preferred over you." (Bukhari, Manaqibu'l-Ansar, 8)

This exceptional moral conduct displayed by the *Ansar* was in fact a step beyond generosity; it was selflessness. Despite having needs of their own, they relentlessly preferred their brethren over themselves. In praise of their mindset, the Almighty reveals:

"And those who made their abode in the city and in the faith before them love those who have fled to them, and do not find in their hearts a need of what they are given, and prefer (them) before themselves though poverty may afflict them, and whoever is preserved from the niggardliness of his soul, these it is that are the successful ones. And those who come after them say: Our Lord! forgive us and those of our brethren who had precedence of us in faith, and do not allow any spite to remain in our hearts towards those who believe, our Lord! surely Thou art Kind, Merciful." (al-Hashr, 9-10)

It was not just the Ansar who had embodied a moral excellence of the kind during the Age of Bliss but also the entire believers, who have likewise been praised by Allah, glory unto Him.[63]

The law of brotherhood established by the Blessed Prophet –upon him blessings and peace- was equally valid during battle. On setting out on a campaign, the Prophet –upon him blessings and peace- would enlist

63 See, al-Insan, 8-11.

one brother into the Muslim army, while leaving the other to see to the needs of both their families and to defend the town if need be.[64]

The below words of Ali –Allah be well-pleased with him- wonderfully reflect the spirit of brotherhood that reigned during the Age of Bliss:

"I can think of two blessings and I do not know which one makes me happier. The first is when someone comes to me with the hope that I might be able to cover his need and genuinely asks for my help. The second is for Allah to take care of his need through me or at least ease his way towards it. I would prefer sorting out the need of a Muslim over a world full of gold and silver." (Ali al-Muttaqi, VI, 598/17049)

In strengthening the brotherly spirit, Anas ibn Malik –Allah be well-pleased with him- would advise his children to "…offer each other presents; for that is the most affective way of increasing your love for each other." (Bukhari, al-Adabu'l-Mufrad, no: 595)

Ibn Abbas -Allah be well-pleased with him- one day entered the *Masjid* for *itiqaf* and greeted another man, assuming a seat on the ground next to him.

"You look tired and upset, my brother", said Ibn Abbas.

---

64 M. Ali Kapar, *Hz. Muhammed'in Müşriklerle Münâsebeti,* İsta - bul 1987, s. 145.

"Yes, indeed so, cousin of the Prophet' he replied. 'So and so had set me free in return for which I am supposed to pay him a certain amount…but by the right of the man (the Prophet) lying in that grave over there, I cannot pay him back."

"Do you want me to have a word to him on your behalf?" asked Ibn Abbas -Allah be well-pleased with him-.

"It is up to you", responded the man. Just as Ibn Abbas -Allah be well-pleased with him- had grabbed his shoes and was making his way out the *Masjid*, the man called out to him:

"Have you forgotten that you are in *itiqaf*?"

"I certainly have not. But let me tell you one thing I heard from the man lying in that grave" said Ibn Abbas -Allah be well-pleased with him-, with tears trickling from his eyes:

"Pursuing and sorting out a brother's need is better than a ten year *itiqaf*…and if one enters *itiqaf* for a day only for the pleasure of Allah, Allah creates between him and Hellfire three ditches…and width of each is as much as that between East and West." (Bayhaki, Shuab'ul-Iman, III, 424-425)

Reminiscing the brotherhood that once was, Ibn Omar –Allah be well-pleased with him- says:

"We saw such times that nobody from among us would ever consider himself more worthy to gold and silver than his fellow brother. And in the times we live in now, gold and silver is more appealing for us than our fellow brethren. I once heard the Messenger of Allah -upon him blessings and peace- say, 'Many a neighbor, in the Hereafter, will grab his other neighbor by the scruff of his neck and plead, 'This neighbor of mine, o Lord, slammed his door to my face and withheld his goodness and help from me.'" (Bukhari, Adabu'l-Mufrad, no: 111; Haythami, X, 285)

The Society was Dominated by Courtesy and Care

The society of the Age of Bliss was one of courtesy and care. Let alone human beings, they were even courteous towards animals and plants, going to utmost measures not to harm anything.

It was especially during pilgrimage that the level of care shown by the Companions' would become vivid. Clothed in *ihram*, the milky white shrouds, they were virtually reaping their share of angelic elegance. While performing the rites of pilgrimage, all Muslims, men and women, would attentively safeguard themselves from vain and imprudent behavior, as the Almighty had commanded, and keep their gazes firmly fixed on their toes, refraining from getting into quarrels of any sort.

Again, for the duration of their period in *ihram*, compliant with the commands of the Lord, they would not even guide a hunter to his game, let alone hunt themselves; even intentionally removing a strand of hair, was something they would refrain from. Though engaging in these activities was permissible at all times else, the fact that they were forbidden during a particular time of pilgrimage, was instilling in their hearts the sense for the need to keep away from all things impermissible and even doubtful. Acting with compassion towards the created for the sake of the Creator, and not hurting any feelings or breaking any hearts, were things they were ever conscious of. This worked towards gradually refining their hearts to the point of elevating them to the peaks of elegance and courtesy, helping them acquire the blend that made them represent the Islam for what it was.

The Blessed Prophet –upon him blessings and peace- would even offer advices on the proper way to tend to animals; he even required that sheep of goats be cleaned of their dust and dirt.[65]

Sawadah ibn Rabi –Allah be well-pleased with him- recounts a magnificent example of compassion at work:

"I visited the Messenger of Allah –upon him blessings and peace- to ask him for a few things. He then requested I be given a few camels (three to ten), and added:

65 Haythami, IV, 66-67.

'When you return home, tell your family to take care of the animals and to feed them properly. Remind them also to keep their nails trimmed so that they do not hurt the animals' breasts while milking them." (Ahmed ibn Hanbal, III, 484; Haythami, V, 168, 259, VIII, 196)

Declaring Medina and its vicinity a *haram*, an inviolable grove, the Blessed Prophet –upon him blessings and peace- said:

"Nobody shall strike the trees inside the grove of Allah and His Messenger with sticks or cut them down. But in the case of need, one may gently shake the leaves down to feed the animals." (Abu Dawud, Hajj, 95-96/2039)

Abu Dushum al-Juhani recounts an incident his father passed onto him from his own father:

"The Messenger of Allah –upon him blessings and peace- once saw a bedouin violently striking his staff against the branches of a tree, to feed its leaves to his livestock.

'Call him over to me', said the Messenger of Allah –upon him blessings and peace-. 'Though gently...do not scare him.'

When the bedouin turned up, the Messenger of Allah –upon him blessings and peace- said to him, 'Shake the branches gently, bedouin, for its leaves to spill...not violently, by force.'

It is as if I can still see the leaves on the bedouin's head." (Ibnu'l-Asir, Usdu'l-Ghabah, Beirut, 1417, VI, 378)

Inviting Muslims to uphold courtesy, consideration and compassion under all circumstances, the Blessed Prophet –upon him blessings and peace- has further said the following about plants:

"There is not a plant that grows on earth that is not protected by the wings of a guardian angel. This continues up until the plant is reaped. Whosoever treads on the plant will incur the curse of the angel." (Ali al-Muttaqi, Kanz, III, 905/9122)

They were Chaste and Virtuous

Chastity and virtue reigned between males and females in the society of the Age of Bliss; for Allah, glory unto Him, had commanded:

"Say to the believing men that they cast down their looks and guard their private parts; that is purer for them; surely Allah is Aware of what they do. And say to the believing women that they cast down their looks and guard their private parts and do not display their ornaments except what appears thereof, and let them wear their head-coverings over their bosoms, and not display their ornaments except to their husbands or their fathers, or the fathers of their husbands, or their sons, or the sons of their husbands, or their brothers, or their brothers' sons, or their sisters' sons, or their women, or those whom their right hands possess, or the male servants not having need (of women), or the children who have not attained knowledge of what is hidden of women; and let them not strike their feet so that what they hide of their ornaments may be known; and turn to Allah all of you, O believers! so that you may be successful." (an-Nur, 30-31)

According to the report of Aisha –Allah be well-pleased with her-, once the above Revelation became known, without waiting to return, the female companions began cutting off the excess fabrics of their clothes to cover their heads and shoulders as had been commanded. (Bukhari, Tafsir, 24/12; Abu Dawud, Libas, 31-33/4102)

Safiyya bint Shaybah –Allah be well-pleased with her- reports that the moment the above Divine command was revealed, the males went home and recited it onto their wives, sisters and daughters. Women, then, turned even their best dresses into headscarves and covered up from head to toe. By doing so, they showed the intensity in which they had embraced and confirmed the Divine command. Come the time of the next *fajr* prayer, women took their places in the rows of the mosque covered from top to bottom. (Ibn Kathir, Tafsir, [an-Nur, 31])

The Companions was extremely sensitive to observe the limits of interaction with the opposite gender. Men and women, who were legally strangers to one another, would not mix with each other in a way that would test those limits. In social life, there was always a distance between men and women and their interaction was regulated by a certain standard and discipline. After all, not only was Islam prohibiting sin, it was also prohibiting behavior and environments that would instigate sinful practice of sin. By putting a distance between Muslims and sinful behavior, Islam was thereby tightly blocking all the roads that would otherwise lead thereto.

Despite placing a great importance on the Friday prayer and offering the other daily ritual prayers in congregation, in order to prevent the mingling of men and women, Islam exempted women from this obligation, suggesting it is more virtuous for them to offer their prayers at home rather than the mosque. The Blessed Prophet –upon him blessings and peace- says:

"The best mosque for women is the corner of their homes." (Ahmed, VI, 297)

Nonetheless, the Noble Messenger –upon him blessings and peace- did not prevent women from attending the mosque and gave permission for those who wanted to do so. Yet, he commanded the women attending not to line up in the same rows as men but in separate rows, behind them.

After each prayer at the mosque, the Blessed Prophet –upon him blessings and peace- would wait and have the male Companions wait awhile, until the female Companions left the mosque and made it to their homes. Only then would they make their way out. Especially after the *fajr* prayer, which was offered before the sun completely broke, the women would shroud themselves in their clothes and head home, without anyone recognizing them. There were even times when they would not recognize each other.[66]

The Noble Messenger –upon him blessings and peace- once suggested they should reserve a certain door of the mosque for the exclusive use of women, after which the male Companions stopped using that door. (Abu Dawud, Salat, 53/571)

Women would also attend the *eid* prayers; yet as usual, their places were at a certain distance from men. Once the Blessed Prophet –upon him blessings and peace- completed his sermon, he would go nearer to the women and give them advice. (Bukhari, Iydayn, 7-8)

Leaving the mosque one day, the Blessed Prophet –upon him blessings and peace- happened to see men

66 See, Bukhari, Adhan, 162-166.

and women inadvertently mixing with each other as they walked, on which he called out to the women to "...walk from the side of the road and not from the middle." Thereupon, women began to walk from beneath the surrounding walls; so much so that their dresses would brush up against them. (Abu Dawud, Adab, 167-168/5272)

Upon seeing men and women mixing with each other during the Umayyad period, Aisha –Allah be well-pleased with her- remarked, "Had the Messenger of Allah –upon him blessings and peace- seen this, he would have forbidden women from entering mosques, just as the Israelites had done." (Bukhari, Adhan, 163)

They Always Had a Smile on their Faces

"Is humor a bad thing?" a man once asked Sufyan ibn Uyaynah –may Allah have mercy on him- (d. 198 AH).

"Much the contrary", he replied, "it is Sunnah; for the Messenger of Allah –upon him blessings and peace- has said, 'I act in humor but I always speak the truth.'" (Nuwayri, Nihayatu'l-Arab fi Fununi'l-Adab, Cairo, IV, 2)

Joking and acting in humor is a prophetic practice. But it must not come at the price of breaking a heart; it should rather be done with the aim of winning one.

Ibn Qayyim al-Jawziyya (d. 751 AH) says:

"The Messenger of Allah –upon him blessings and peace- would act in humor, though he would always utter the truth. There was metonymy in his speech it was always used to express the truth." (Ibn Qayyim al-Jawziyya, Zadu'l-Maad, I, 58)

The Companions were lively and joyful people, who knew what to say and where to say it. At times witty and humorous, they were also serious and somber when needed. Their lives struck a perfect balance, free of excess.

Bakr ibn Abdullah –Allah be well-pleased with him- says:

"The Companions would joke with each other, using watermelons at times. But when a serious situation arose, they would get serious and take great pains to see to the task." (Bukhari, al-Adabu'l-Mufrad, no: 266)

Abu Salamah ibn Abdurrahman –Allah be well-pleased him- depicts the Companions as follows:

"The Companions were never ones to laze and shrink back. They would recite poems in their gatherings and tell each other stories of their days of Ignorance. But when any one of them was faced with a duty surrounding the religion of Allah, his eyes would virtually fly out of his sockets out of desperation to fulfill it." (Bukhari, al-Adabu'l-Mufrad, no: 555)

Thabit ibn Ubayd explains:

"I have never seen anyone more solemn than Zayd ibn Thabit; though neither have I seen anyone chattier than him at home." (Bukhari, al-Adabu'l-Mufrad, no: 286)

After observing a bedouin praying, after performing a really quick ritual prayer, "Wed me, Lord, to the *houri*s of Paradise!" Omar –Allah be well-pleased with him- humorously remarked:

"Man…that is so much to ask for so little a price!"

According to report of Abu Bạkr as-Saqafi, the Companions would alternate between reading the Quran and poetry. (Kattani, at-Taratib, II, 236)

When with his students, Ibn Abbas –Allah be well-pleased with him- would narrate a few *ahadith*, and then say:

"Whet our appetites with some jokes or a few lines of poetry; for the spirit is prone to becoming weary just like the body." He would, at times, follow this up by recounting some classical parables renowned by the Arabs, after which he would resume the lesson, repeating this procedure whenever the need would arise. (Kattani, at-Taratib, II, 237)

On saying anything whatsoever, Abu'd-Darda –Allah be well-pleased with him- would make sure to smile. One day, his wife told him, "I fear people might get the wrong impression."

"But", replied he, "there was always a smile in the Prophet's –upon him blessings and peace- speech." (Ahmed, V, 198, 199)

Abdullah ibn Muhammad, of the *Tabiun* generation, was a jovial and humorous man. Even watching her aunt Aisha –Allah be well-pleased with her- in her deathbed did not deter him from making a joke. It is reported that he visited her during her final illness, where he asked:

"How do you feel my dearest aunt?"

"I assure you", she replied, "this sure is the throes of death".

"In that case", he remarked, "it cannot be that serious!" Astounded to see him carry on his jokes even amid such a setting, Aisha –Allah be well-pleased with her- said:

"By Allah, it seems you will kick your habit!" (Ibn Saad, VIII, 76)

In Short

The Blessed Prophet –upon him blessings and peace- was a mercy not only for entire humankind but also for the entire universe. His wonderful appearance on Earth illumined its pitch dark horizons, signaling the dawning of a brand new day which humanity had been anticipating. Hearts were unlocked, eyes were opened; the murky flow of life was rinsed spotless. Through the showers of his blessings, the universe reached an eternal spring. Man was united with his true honor and the justice he had been yearning for; it was the Prophet –upon him blessings and peace- who gave him the insight into the mystery of life and eternity.

That great Prophet hailed from an unlettered society; yet, the Grand Book revealed to him became the guiding lamp to the books on the dusty library shelves. A downpour of wisdom onto thirsty hearts, it was the opening lesson of 'true knowledge', setting the standard for lessons to follow.

It was again that Prophet of Mercy who opened the pages of the grand book that is the universe. He became the translator of languages silent and unknown; languages forever busy in the remembrance of Allah, glory unto Him. By guiding many a society previously struggling in a bestial life to its true honor and dignity, he became the king of love enthroned right in the hearts of the guided.

The Almighty had the model of an exemplary human being embodied in the Blessed Prophet –upon him blessings and peace-, making him the quintessential example for entire humanity. Good morals, which consist of nothing but the behavior and conduct that please the Lord, was thereby conveyed to mankind through the exemplary words and conduct of the Blessed Prophet –upon him blessings and peace-.

In fact, when asked about the morals of the Blessed Prophet –upon him blessings and peace-, Aisha –Allah be well-pleased with her- simply replied, "His morals were that of the Quran". (Muslim, Musafirin, 139)

The Blessed Prophet –upon him blessings and peace- was 'the Quran come-to-life'. His life was the practical interpretation of the Quran that had been revealed to his pure heart. In honoring his towering morals, the Almighty declares:

"Nay, verily for you is a Reward unfailing. And you stand on an exalted standard of character." (al-Qalam, 3-4)

The Blessed Prophet –upon him blessings and peace- is the grandest pillar of morality ever witnessed by humankind. And his most loyal followers are the Companions and then the righteous. Believers, who have rejoiced the value of treading his path, have also acquired outstanding characters, worthy of the honor and name of man.

It was for immersing their hearts in the love of the Noble Messenger –upon him blessings and peace- and obeying him under all circumstances that the Companions embodied the prophetic morals and received thereby the praises of Allah, glory unto Him. The Quran in fact states:

"And the first to lead the way, of the *Muhajirun* and the *Ansar*, and those who followed them in goodness - Allah is well pleased with them and they are well pleased with Him, and He hath made ready for them Gardens underneath which rivers flow, wherein they will abide for ever. That is the supreme triumph." (at-Tawbah, 100)

We no longer have the opportunity to become Companions. Yet, as the *ayah* declares, 'following them in goodness' and in doing so, acquiring the pleasure of the Lord is an opportunity that remains with us so long as we are alive.

The best to reflect the morals of the Blessed Prophet –upon him blessings and peace- throughout the centuries following the Companions, have been the righteous saints, designated as examples by the Almighty Himself:

"Now surely the friends of Allah- they shall have no fear nor shall they grieve" (Yunus, 62). They evidently enjoy a privileged rank in Divine sight; to reap a share of this Divine guarantee, it is therefore best to follow their path.

Since the Companions and saints were able to become one with the Prophet's –upon him blessings and peace- character by acquiring an immense share therefrom, all the beauty of conduct they were able to exhibit throughout their lives, are nothing but reflections mirrored by the Prophet's –upon him blessings and peace- own exemplary character. Wherever there is beauty, it is but a reflection from *him*. Not a flower booms through the soil that is not from *his* light. It is because of *him* that we are. He is a bloom of pure light from the Divine that never wilts and only appears fresher with each passing moment.

In the footsteps of the Companions and the righteous Muslims who followed, we are compelled to fill our existence with the love of the Prophet –upon him blessings and peace- and seek to embody his superb morals. We must strive to live and revive those beauties that are timeless despite the passage of centuries. This is the price for being a worthy devotee of the Blessed Prophet –upon him blessings and peace-.

Endless thanks to the Lord for rendering us members of the Blessed Prophet's –upon him blessings and peace- nation, free of charge. Yet, the path to infiltrating into the core of this Divine grace and to becoming worthy of the Prophet's love and his compliment of us as 'his brothers', runs through embracing his *Sunnah* and embodying his morals.

Comprehensively grasping the wonder of creation that is the Blessed Prophet –upon him blessings and peace- and his sublime morality, and articulating it within the limited scope of human language is in fact impossible. The sensory impressions we receive from the world, on which our thinking depends, would fall hopelessly short of the task; just as it is utterly impossible to fit the entire ocean into a cup. What has spilled forth from our tongues in trying to explain both him and the Age of Bliss is therefore nothing but crumbs reflected forth from his inexplicable beauty.

Lord…Grant our hearts a share of the sublime morals and spirituality of Your Noblest Messenger! Let our hearts reverberate in the sound of those who used to cry out, 'may our parents be ransomed for you, Messenger of Allah!

Amin

Contents